Devil You Can't Have My Child!

A Story Of Redemption

Ken Johnson

Devil You Can't Have My Child!

Printed in USA by 48HrBooks (www.48HrBooks.com)

Acknowledgements

I want to say thank you to my wife, who has been my biggest supporter and fan through the good times and the bad. I want to thank my kids for loving their father unconditionally and to my mother and mother in-law for being two of the sweetest people in the world. I also want to thank my Aunt Wendy for always being there for me, and to my family and my church family, which are far too many to name. Thanks for being there for me. I love you all!

I want to give a special thanks to Pastors Denorvice Howard, Pastor Lennell Caldwell, and Pastor Don Couch for being wonderful examples of what real Men of God are supposed to look like. You're examples of being faithful pastors, husbands and fathers, set a wonderful foundation for the life I now live. God bless you.

A special thanks goes out to my pastors the apostles, Mom and Dad Carter of Sanctuary Evangelistic Church in Tulsa, Oklahoma. Your wisdom, guidance, and love are amazing. You have been a rock to me in some very turbulent times and for that I say thank you.

To every pastor, minister, friend, and associate whom I didn't call by name you're too numerous to name and the impact you've made is too great to be contained in this one writing. However, I want to say thank you for every kind word, prayer, and thoughtful gesture. I love you from the depths of my soul, and the seeds you have planted in my life and ministry will be remembered forever.

To Damon James, my best friend forever, I just want to say thank you publicly for being my true friend.

Your honesty and your integrity have helped guide me in many critical moments in my life.

I'll never forget your words of wisdom when I thought I was the super saint who would never make a mistake again after being filled with the Holy Spirit. You told me, "Ken, when you make a mistake (and I did), remember, He still saw fit to save you. He knows your future better than you know your past and He still saves us in spite of us.

To my aunts Judy and Michelle to my grandparents Esther and Mansfield to My momma Dean to those who have ran there race and gone on to be with the Lord I am forever grateful for the seeds of wisdom Love and Generosity that you sowed into my Life!

Thank You!

Chapter 1- Chief Of The Sinners

1st Timothy 1:15 – This is a faithful saying, and worthy of all acceptation, that Christ Jesus came into the world to save sinners; of whom I am chief.

I know I was bad and I'm not talking about teen or adolescent bad, I'm talking about there was resident evil in my life, Chucky bad, an unseen force working in the crevices of my soul. I don't know how the door was opened! Did it come from the movies I watched? Or the blood that ran through my veins All I know is that I had an inclination from my early youth to always do evil. Selling drugs came natural for me violence was easy for me. It was like I was born to be a hustler. I remember my first experience with selling drugs very clearly. I had gotten a large amount of marijuana before I was thirteen from my step father Darnell. I remember the feelings of excitement it was like I had gotten a free pass to Cedar Point for a week. I was excited to sit down and to guess how much weight to put in the bag. I didn't need a scale. I was going on sheer instinct. My adrenaline flowing, my mind racing.

My expectations of becoming wealthy beyond my wildest dreams coming to pass, I could see myself like the street legends of my day. Wearing big gold chains and troop jackets riding on vogues and wells on my Cadillac being whispered about everywhere I went. I could see them saying that's Chip. He's a hustler, he has money, he's a bad man, he's crazy and you better not mess with his stuff. All this in a mind that had been shaped to be a criminal from the womb. I grew up in a family of hustlers a neighborhood filled with want to be kingpins. This book is my story, it's not a knock against anyone in my family who raised me. I believe beyond a shadow of a doubt they did the best they could in their minds, considering the time and the era they grew up in. It's amazing as a child in the 70's and 80's. I never heard people use glowing terms talking with their kids or grand kids like I love you. You're going to be a success in life. You're going to make it big. Those words came later, much later and they came from people who couldn't love me and I did not love them. They thought they loved me because I gave them things and I thought they loved me because they gave me sex. Boy I was wrong. In any event my early childhood was marred with the wrong types of affirmation.

I was either called out of my name with words like "you white honky, or b----, you'll never be nothing that one stuck with me for a while it actually became my players anthem and response to every female I got into confrontation with to be called a stupid Mother F' was common and consistent". I heard from people who had been wounded in their childhood. "I wish you would have died on the operating table, I knew I should have gotten an abortion, I hate you, I hate the day you were born." My life always came with the constant threat of being dropped off at Metzenbaums, the detention center for wayward kids or parents who just couldn't take the pressures of raising children. So many kids just got dropped off there when their parents just couldn't cope with being a parent. I heard a lot of things growing up not all of it was bad but most of it was.

Ghetto slang was natural, trying to be cool was natural (whatever cool is), getting cussed out was a normal occurrence. After a while it just becomes a part of who you are, you have faith to receive a cussing out daily. I saw a lot of violence growing up I was violent beyond belief so violent the death locks gang members named me after a fictional character call Lu-can who was a wild cave child. I would pick fights with kids in the neighborhood, boys walking down the streets I had never met.

I would run up to them and start swinging hay-makers at their heads just because they were in my neighborhood without permission.

I saw Parents fighting each other I've seen weddings turn into blood baths literally where an enraged cousin would beat his wife into bloody submission. I saw men belittled and humiliated, called every foul name in the book. I saw grown men being told to shut up and go sit down. I saw men mugged by women who would rip the very essence of their manhood out of them by women who were angry at times, who were very controlling, very manipulating. I have been the accomplice of a many cheat sessions where I would be taken out of the house to be used as an excuse for women to see their other lovers. I have also seen these same men come to a place in their lives where they stood up for a moment for their manhood and dignity not responding with kindness and walking in love but on many occasions they had blood on their mind and revenge in their hearts.

I saw women who were the assassins and killers of men souls find themselves in positions where they were being choked to death and having their very life ooze out of them. I have witnessed domestic violence to the degree where if my brother and I had not jumped into what seemed like warranted payback fights at the time, we would have buried our mother decades ago. Words are very powerful weapons, especially in the hands of untrained people. Words are so powerful because they shape the psychology of every person that exists on this planet. Words are containers – they contain your life; your victories; and your defeats. Words shape the worlds in which we live in today. Words hold our universe together and the systems God has put in place in the atmospheric heavens.

Hebrews 1:3 "Who being the brightness of his glory, and the express image of his person, and upholding all things by the word of his power;"

Whether you believe it or not, words have power!

What we listen to shapes our minds. I listened to NWA growing up. I sang songs day and night like dope man dope man f- the police and what I sang day and night it shaped my mind those words shaped my life. Whether it's talk radio, talk shows or the news, words spoken into your life and over your life they shape your life. Your favorite singer is shaping your life and your kids lives. Katie Perry saying I kissed a girl and I liked it is shaping some girl or woman's life. There is nothing wrong with a little bump and grind by R-Kelly is shaping someone's life. Words will cause good people to have one night stands. Words will cause you to meet that special someone words are powerful! Words shape how you look at people. I have seen some beautiful women with some ugly men and I've asked questions on how he pulled that one off and she would say he talked to me nicely he said the right things? Before there was great sex there was a great conversation. If you will allow yourself to like people, it is determined by the amount of words you speak and they speak. The more you keep talking; it determines if we go out again or if he or she is not for me. Words bind us together contractually whether it's verbal or written. Words will get you married, "I do", the right words will keep you married and the wrong words will cause justices around the world to say that half your belongings belong to the one who you previously said "I do" to. Words impacted the beginning of my life in a very negative way and throughout my entire life my words have shaped my realities. I remember growing up and having this reality that most people I knew would end up in prison. I always said things like I know I'm going to jail. I know when I get caught they're going to give me some serious time.

I was the prophet of gloom and doom over my own life to the degree that when I got busted for the first and only time, I didn't get probation. I got seven years in the penal system. Why? Because crime does pay. It just pays negatively. Secondly, I said I was a hustler, I said I was a criminal; I said I was going to jail and everything I said became a self-fulfilling prophecy. I never got caught selling drugs, using a pistol or with a trunk full of money. As a matter of fact, the only thing that locked me up was my words on a taped phone conversation. Don't tell me words are not powerful. Words in the hands of a Johnny Cochran, the right words caused OJ Simpson to go free. Words in the hands of President Bush caused Saddam's kingdom to fall and the words coming out of your mouth will either free you up or bring you into bondage. Listen to the authority believers have to take words and to legislate what they allow or disallow to happen in their lives.

Matthew 16:19 – And I will give unto thee the keys of the kingdom of heaven: and whatsoever thou shalt bind on earth shall be bound in heaven: and whatsoever thou shalt loose on earth shall be loosed in heaven.

The only way we bind or declare what is unlawful is with our words and the only way we lose or declare what is lawful is with our words. Words will change everything about you if used in the right manner. This book is written not just to show you the power of the spoken word but this book is written to show you that the Word (Jesus) can change the worst of mankind. I'm not a Hebrew or Greek scholar. I'm simply a man who has been changed by the power of God. *"I truly am God taking the foolish things of this world to confound the wise; But God hath chosen the foolish things of the world to confound the wise; and God hath chosen the weak things of the world to confound the things which are mighty;" 1st Corinthians 1:27*

Please come into a world I lived in for more than half of my life. It is brutally honest, and explicitly graphic. For some, you will cry, others will laugh, for all it will be a time to see that God still has the power to change the hearts of lost men! God, still has the power to take men from the gutter to the utmost.

Chapter 2 - Why is God Angry

As a 6 year old child, my mind was very attentive to small details. I asked a lot of questions. I had a lot of questions on my mind. Why did my mother leave me with Mommy? Who were my grandmother and Daddy? Who was my grandfather? Why didn't she want us? Why didn't she want me? What did I do to make her run away from us? Didn't my mother know that we longed to see her face daily? I couldn't imagine why my mother would abandon us. Didn't she know that my brother, Kevin, was a great kid? He did his best to take care of his little brother. He had the assignment of shaping my mind at a young age. He taught me how to put a crease in my jeans, he instructed me on how to clean the house, he showed me how to wash my first batch of dishes and he taught me how to survive in a kitchen. I would have never known bread fried in butter was just as good as French toast, and that government cheese made the most incredible cheese toast sandwiches and that government peanut butter really wasn't that bad if you melted it first and then spread it. I would have never known the dozens of different ways you could fry a potato, he showed me how to make French fries, home fries, home fries with cheese, home fries with sausage and many other incredible delights he would make us from the one constant that could be found in the house and that was a bag of potatoes. Kevin was my hero. He taught me how to play football, he broke my collar bone teaching me to wrestle at the YMCA, and he taught me how to fight and how to survive in the ghetto.

He gave me my first drink of Old English beer. Kevin taught me the forbidden world of sexual pleasure as he would have me to look and listen to his sexual escapades through holes in the walls. The keyhole would be my choice on most occasions when he was taking care of sexual business when my parents would be out doing their runs. I was so amazed at what I saw and as a child I never understood why they made noises as though they were fighting for survival in the rumble from the jungle. My brother was the man. I loved him and I still do, but my brother never admitted he longed to know who his father was, who he has never seen. We both just acted like our fathers never existed like we just got here as thought the storks dropped us off. He never admitted he wanted to see our mother while she was out of our life; he just made the most of his life as best a child could he tried to become a man before his time and being the man always meant having sex with something or somebody. I don't know how this door was open but I do know my brother was into trying to fit himself into anybody he could penetrate his way into. It didn't matter if it was a female who looked like grape ape or him trying to rub on his light skin brothers' behind, squeezing it and rubbing it as though it was a football getting ready to be thrown to a tight end. I don't know what happened. I do know that as much as I have tried to block out my brothers action against me, I do remember my own brother trying to have sex with me not even understanding what was going on. I just remember his approach treating it like little kids playing house let me do this, let me try to put my dick inside of you, it won't hurt , it's going to feel good.

You know I wouldn't hurt you, you're my little brother and yes big brother you are my Hero. And even though I can never remember sexual penetration on this occasion I do remember the incident very clearly it was the middle room in the house that jack built on a mattress that laid in the middle of the floor as our bed, My brother humped on me I cannot say it ever happened again but that day happened it was real and I make no excuses for his actions its over it happened but what happens behind closed doors affects many people lives openly. My brother has his own deviant set of issues, his own abandonment issues. I'm not his judge I am his brother. On many occasions I have tried to be there for him but with one issue comes another and about the time Mom came back to get us in 1980, his experiments in too many things became vices and addictions that have haunted him since our youth.

It started with 40 ounces of beer but it's been a 28 year battle with crack that has been on and running since he first experimented with crack at 16 at the hand of a family member who didn't think it crazy or strange to give a boy a drug that the oldest of adults couldn't handle. My years as a child growing up with my brother are mixed reviews. He took me as far as he could. He fed me, he tried to do me a favor and teach me about sex when we got older he tried to get me my first piece of trim in the sixth grade but I was too scared and I didn't know what to do so I backed out of the sex-escapade he had put in place because of fear. I will always see the picture though when I think about my brother as little men being held in daddy's arms, he was the beautiful chocolate baby and I was the one nearly white but neither of us knew anything that day in daddy's arms but love, smiles and happiness. That picture of the brother I lost will always be etched in my heart. My love has changed for him. It has actually grown. I understand that he is not his actions although responsible for the voices he listens to; he is not a failure even though he has failed repeatedly. He is not the mistakes he has made even though he has made thousands of them. My brother is a man, God sees as forgiven washed in the blood of Jesus Christ whose addictions lead him instead of the Holy Spirit. I was called one day and informed that my brother had been shot several times. I was now an adult who had an encounter with Christ. It was my duty to go and pray for my brother and to believe God for his recovery. I entered into the hospital after a few days of contemplation and prayer. I went with one of my cousins, Reggie, who had recently been converted to Christ. I asked Reggie to go with me and to pray with me for Kevin's miracle. When I got there my step father was in the room with him. I noticed he was conscious, his wounds weren't as life threatening as my family had made it. I began to minister to my brother about the love of Jesus. I began to talk with him about how God loved him, even after all that he had done to ruin his life and others. He was never a good father to the several kids he had fathered. He had dealt them blow after blow of unfaithfulness but I wanted to make sure he knew that after all of the robberies and all of the seduction and all of the lying and cheating, that the God I served loved him and would give him a second chance. Kevin had been shot 5 times and survived. He was a man with nine lives. He had been beaten on several occasions nearly to death for stealing crack from drug dealers.

He had been shot at several times without being hit, he had stayed in abandoned homes, slept with anything he could, would lie to a woman to stay in her house and then rob her blind of her possessions and her heart. He was a natural deviant, but God still saw fit to take what was worthless in my eyes and give him the greatest gift in life. I ministered to a man my flesh hated but my spirit loved and God showed up in the midst of our dysfunction. Kevin gave his heart to Jesus in a hospital room at Huron Road hospital and not only did God save him but while he laid in a hospital bed God had me lay hands on him and the Lord filled Kevin with the Holy Spirit with the evidence of speaking in other tongues as the Bible declares in Acts chapter 2 and they were all filled with the Holy Spirit and began to speak in other tongues as the spirit gave them utterance, and it was a powerful deliverance that hit my brothers spirit.

I was more in amazement than shock at the depth of God's love. In my eyes Kevin didn't deserve anything. In Gods eyes Kevin deserved it all and not only did he save Kevin that day, he saved Darnell. After seeing the power of God hit Kevin, Darnell asked us would you please give me this Jesus whom you preach so passionately about. I want to be saved too. I'm so glad that I obeyed the Lord that day because God saved both of them. Darnell would later die from a heart attack that I cannot say was directly related to drugs but what I can say is I have seen God save people who have issues who have done the whole world a disservice but His love for His people is always greater than their issues. I would, just a few years ago, be the minister at Darnell's funeral but I am still a brother to a man whom Jesus loves who loves crack more than he loves God but Kevin is not his issue. He is a son of God who like many of us still has issues even though you have God. My relationship with Kevin has been tested several times since the hospital incident. I actually gave him a job working for me at a restaurant. He did great for a few days, then he relapsed and came one night and broke into the restaurant stole the food and the mobile food truck. He goes out on a crack induced binge that cost me several hundreds of dollars in repair fees. He destroyed the iron gate at the restaurant and the column on the steering wheel. He has done countless acts against me after salvation but my love for him is greater than his fleshly hatred for me.

I have seen many acts of other people's pain played out in my life. I have been the butt of too many jokes. I have been called too many names by people that you call family and friends and yet, I have no enemies, only confused friends. My heart refuses to hate who I should hate and to hurt who I should hurt. God has been incredibly good to me, even when I didn't know His name He still kept me and shielded me from the death and abortion of a great life in Christ that the enemy was and is still trying to bring into play.

I grew up in a very small house with very giant attitudes. My grandmother was small but she carried a big stick and she could hold her liquor like the greats from Maverick. My granny would have get-togethers on a regular basis. There was always somebody stopping by with a bottle of Ole Grand Mcnish or some other liquor. My grandmother had some friends from Massillon, Ohio who would stop by a couple of times a year and they would on occasion spend the night if it got too late and they got too drunk to drive. I loved Ernestine and her son, big Chip. He was fun to be around and I bore his name even though he wasn't my father he was light and bright and big and burly just like I was. Big Chip was my friend and I loved him like he was family.

I actually called his mom Auntie. It's like a tradition in the black community if a person stops by the house a few times and they are older than you they become your kinfolk. My fake cousin, Big Chip was fun to be around. He was cool but he was also a pervert and in the mind of a 7 year old child who has never had sex but has been humped previously yet not understanding I was violated I am now placed in the bed with a man who is told to come and sleep in my bed so he could get some rest before the ride back to Massillon in the morning. It's late and we are dozing off to sleep when I feel this man rubbing on me and telling me he is not going to hurt me. I wonder why people who are out to hurt you always declare this is not going to hurt. My cousin Big Chip begins to tell me how much he loves me and would never hurt me and as a matter of fact tomorrow I'm going to buy you some ice cream when the ice cream truck comes down the street if you let me touch you. If you let me rub you I won't hurt you. Let me hump you I won't put it in. I just want to rub you. The thought never entered my mind as a child of how wrong this really is. I remember my brother wanted to rub me. Now my play cousin wants to rub me. Both of these men really loved me and I wanted to be accepted by them because this must be what men do to little boys. This must be natural, I thought in my mind. I didn't know the enemy was trying to open up a door of deception or seduction in my life. I never once guessed the devil himself was trying to plant a seed that would destroy me or cause great sexual deviancy. It's funny but the people who knew better did nothing in the morning. After Big Chip's humping session, my brother while in the backyard told all of my cousins I had sold my soul for some ice cream. The villain who saw the villain never sought to protect me. He sought to belittle me. It's amazing how the devil will set you up and then shame you by those who should love you and protect you. Life will never give you what you deserve. It will, many times offer hurt, guilt, and shame. To a child's mind I could only think what I did to deserve all of this pain. When it rained, I would run to the living room window and watch the darkness descend over the earth. I would listen to the sounds of the thunder and lightning shaking the heavens and I would say I guess God is mad again. I wonder was it something I did to make him angry with me!

Chapter 3 - Trick Baby

I was always a very inquisitive kid. I asked a lot of questions mainly to a quiet audience like any kid coming of age and understanding the natural order of life. I wanted to know who my father was. I would pop the question on occasion amongst family. Who is my daddy? Does anyone know him? It's amazing the broad range of answers that was given. He was the grocery store owner down the street, he was the variety store owner up the street, whoever he was I know he wasn't black and I am absolutely positive he wasn't short because I am light nearly white with curly hair and standing tall at 6 foot 3 inches.

I don't think like most people from my family or my neighborhood. My genes think at all times on how to do business. I assume that my father was a business man naturally just because of the natural inclinations that run through my veins. I can sit down and within an hour create concepts that will win in the market place yet I'm not the greatest manager. I have incredible creative skills. I see success in my mind; I understand how it's supposed to look. I can create a business with no money and have it running in 30 days. I think differently. I look different. But the day I found my birth certificate it would not matter who appeared at the door. I had struck gold. I had a name that I could put with my heritage. I had a man that could be attached to my birth. I remember finding the birth certificate. I saw my name, my mother's name and Charles Guess. I ran down the stairs in excitement like the little kids from Little House on the Prairie running to the dinner table for a meal with the family. I ran into the living room, “Ma I have found my birth certificate and who is this man that is marked as my father Charles Guess.” My mother looked amazed that I had found this precious jewel and she began to tell me of his legacy and who he was and what he had accomplished. As I listened to the story of this amazing man’s life I was in awe, he was a hustler, a drug dealer, a player, a pimp, and so much more. He was a kingpin who had it all. Money, houses, cars, jewelry, clothes, women and he was my father. I thought the God who had been mad at me all of those years had now found mercy for my life. I had a father and he was rich, he was everything I wanted to be: a drug dealing, womanizing, high rolling player.

I asked my mother if she could introduce me to him. She said she didn't have any way of getting in contact with him. My heart sank for a moment but then she said your auntie Judy knows him well. Maybe she can introduce him to you. I quickly called my auntie who I knew wouldn't withhold any good thing from me. I was already a son to her and she was already a mother to me. Judy was the apple of my eye since the first day I had met her in the late 70s rocking a one piece body suit. She was fun to be around, young, beautiful well dressed, energetic, lively, to say the least and she too was an amazing hustler. Auntie would pull up with stacks of money and driving the finest cars and she would always make time for the son she never had whom I had become. I had become sort of a dreamer at a young age. I would see things and then go to the numbers dream books and find out what the number was so that I could pass it on to my favorite aunt/mother. I had dreamed several things that translated into hits. I saw myself on an airplane on one occasion and went to the dream book and gave my Judy the number 317 and she had hit for thousands. I was the house prophet and didn't know it. I was a seer or as the family said I had the gift of E.S.P. (Extra Sensory Perception). On many occasions I could see something in my dream, translate it into a number which would translate into cash. Judy was never cheap even without a number but after the big hit she flushed me with two hundred dollar bills and for a kid in the 80s I was rich. I quickly would cash a hundred dollar bill into smaller bills to fatten up my bankroll. I was rolling. I waited for the day Judy would stop by after finding my birth certificate. I ran excitedly into her arms and asked her who is this man Charles Guess on my birth certificate and she looked at me and smiled and said I know him and I will introduce you to him. My heart fell to my feet as excitement ran through my veins. I was going to meet the man who had given me life and I was glad about it. A few days later, the meeting had been set. Charles was coming to get his boy. I had no animosity that he had been out of my life my whole life. I was not angry, I did not care. I had a father who was coming to pick me up. I was instructed to be ready; he would be there to pick me up at 5 pm. I waited at the door patiently lips dry with the excitement of seeing my father. The nervous energy was too much to bear. I was dehydrated from nervous excitement. 5 pm came he wasn't there. 5:30 came. I was sweating bullets, and thinking where are you daddy, don't you know your boy is at the window waiting for you. 6:15 arrives and he pulls up in his 735 BMW. I am floored I am getting to meet my father and he has a BMW. I ran to the car jumped in the front seat, he pulls off the street and we are now in motion. Life has changed; I am with my father after 14 years of silence. I couldn't shut up. "What do I call you Sir, Charles, or daddy what?" He says you can call me Chuck. We drove around for hours talking. I had a million questions he answered them as well as someone could who had just been thrown into the face of having another child presented to them unexpectedly. I will never forget one answer that I received. I asked the question, "Are you really my daddy?" He gave me the most confusing answer I had ever heard. "Well yes chronologically I am your father but not biologically." I didn't understand that at all as he began to fumble around the answer as politely as he could. What he was trying to say was I was there when you were born but you're not actually my seed. I signed the birth certificate, making myself liable but if we ran some test I may not come up as the match. I didn't care if this was beginning to sound like Jerry Springer at noon. All l cared about is that he said "yes I am your daddy." I heard and understood that part well; the other clinical terms were fuzzy to a fourteen year old who was living in a nostalgic state because he had a father. No man, no woman, no one would steal this moment from me. After fourteen years I was about to get mine as a son of one of the most powerful drug dealers the city had ever seen. We rode that day and established a relationship. I poured out my soul to him. I told him who I was and what I did. I was a boxer preparing for the junior Olympics who would one day fight in the golden gloves and go off to win the gold at the Olympics which would eventually turn me into a world renown pro. In my mind I had it all figured out. I would be the next great fighter of the century to follow in the footsteps of my hero the great Sugar Ray Leonard. Although my boxing career never panned out, I lost more fights than I won, for a few hours I told the man I had dreamed of meeting my whole life the story I envisioned for my life.

That night I was marked as I rode with Chuck. He took me into suburban homes; he exposed me to more than I had ever seen in a few hours time. I had seen him collect money, talk privately to beautiful women and we were riding in luxury. It didn't matter that when I looked at him, he was as short as George Jefferson and, as dark as JJ from good times his hair was as kinky as Kunta Kente from Roots. I had a father who didn't look like me but I wanted to be like him. For nearly two years I would spend time with him nearly every week. I would meet him at our inner-city drop house and I would be whisked off to the penthouses of Lakeshore and Mayfield to live the Willis and Gary Coleman life for a few days out of each week. I was now in charge of washing all of my daddy's cars. He didn't just throw hundred dollar bills at me he made me work for it. I would be washing limousines and Porsches, Cadillac's, Mercedes, Corvettes, Acura Legends, and Audi's you name it, he had it and I was in charge of keeping all of these cars clean that were spaced out over the parking lot in this massive complex. I didn't mind the hard work even though it became tedious over time but I did enjoy when I got paid at the end of my workday. My daddy would give me several hundred dollars for taking care of his fleet of cars and to a kid who's not even 15 yet I was living the life. Every time my cousins would see me, they would be amazed at how my life had changed. I had gone from buying 50 cents worth of shaved bologna with them on the weekends, eating King Vitamin cereal to every time we would go into a store or pass an eatery I had money to spare. I was balling out of control. I was in an euphoric place that I never wanted to end. I had a father who loved me, he loved me so much that he had allowed me to spend the night most weekends; he would allow me to ride with him as his body guard. I thought in mind at least I was his protector, he gave me the privilege of carrying his cell phone that was so big it had to be put in a brief case and it was heavy but I loved being seen carrying that cell phone brief case. The ladies loved cool Chip, I was the man. I really believed in my heart that I was accepted and loved. Chuck gave me the privilege of staying with him the summer of 1987. I was 15 years old, I was responsible. I did whatever was asked of me on a daily basis whether it was cleaning the penthouse, washing the cars, working at the garage, learning how to sand cars at his body shop or carrying his cell phone, with love. In my mind, I had become an asset to my father's empire.

The summer was coming to a close when my father informed me I could live with him and go to school from his house. I was excited to say the least. I would be able to live with my father; I would get a chance to become a real man hanging under the wing of a man I idolized. He was rich beyond anything I had ever seen, he was the wisest man I had ever known. I was being trained to be a Muslim activist as we watched and listened to Farrakhan and Dick Gregory constantly, he had stacks of videos and audio tapes, and he was shaping my mind. There was no God but Allah and Muhammad was his messenger. I was lost in an euphoric state. I was eating at Lancers and there were frog legs and shrimps daily in the house. I was swimming in the pool at the lower levels of the towers. I was living in a penthouse with a man who had a board filled with over a hundred keys that represented cars and houses that he owned everywhere. I witnessed women who would sit around the penthouse six or more at a time inside of the same house without an argument. They knew each other, they had kids by him, some sold his drugs and were his ladies of pleasure and we would all sit eat and drink together, watching Farrakhan on the big screen we were a family. He would call the ladies up to his room one at a time or several at a time. I don't think it was just for sexual pleasure because ladies made him rich they were the money makers of the organization and all of them felt like they were his woman but at the end of the day all of them used each other. He was a master motivator he used drugs, power and money to persuade the masses, he was no low level pusher he helped to fuel a big economy he brought cars from the biggest dealerships in the city, Motorcars of Cleveland was his main car dealership to shop at. We would walk into the general managers' office with bags of money he was the Scarface of the city and I was his proud son the up and coming heir to the throne. I couldn't count the days fast enough to reach sixteen. I was promised an Italian Fiat car brand new for a penny a week. I was next in line for a blessing. My life had changed, my boxing career had fizzled. I was too cute now to take a punch. I was focused quietly on taking over my daddy's empire as soon as I could get my license and could show him how responsible I was in picking up and dropping off for him. I knew most of his connects. I knew most of the dealers. I wanted to be my father's reliable son. The other brothers I met were needy and clingy although they were older, they didn't have the empire on their mind. They wanted temporary fixes, a few dollars, a shot of whiskey, a hit of cocaine. I wanted long term success. I was delusional at a young age but aggressive. I had already started selling monkey paw marijuana. I was the man before sixteen and now I am called to live in the palace. My father has given me the green light to move into the penthouse. School is quickly approaching. I knew that it would be time for me to shop as I had done in years gone by. The previous year I was given seven thousand dollars to go school shopping with and a plane ticket to New York City for me and my favorite aunt Judy to go shopping in the Big Apple. I figured in my mind this year he is at least going to give me ten stacks. Daddy hadn't taken me shopping yet but on the first day of school at Shaw High I was given instructions to go to Shaw to finalize my transfer and I would be enrolled in a private school called St. Joseph's right down the street from our penthouse. I was blown away. I would be going to one of the top high schools in the city. I followed instructions. I got my transfer. I went to our safe house for pick up in Cleveland by my daddy. The safe house was a place where only a few people could come to. It was filled with money drops from the day. It was a meeting place for him and his main girl. I waited anxiously for him to get there. I was ready to go to the big house. I was ready to go to my new school I was living with my daddy. Life was perfect. In two weeks I would be sixteen. I am getting a new car my future is bright.

Its Thursday Night the football game is on the big screen, we are relaxing waiting to leave when we hear a beating at the door. Someone is banging on it uncontrollably. It can't be my dad he has keys. I run to see who it is, not knowing if it's the feds or a friend. It's Amin, he is beating the door down screaming, but he's screaming the most horrific words I had ever heard in my life. "Chuck is dead. Chuck is dead. Chuck is dead. He was just shot and killed right down the street on Olhman." The words hit me like a drunk driver in a head on collision. I sank to the floor and cried as I had never cried all the days of my life. "Daddy, daddy, no daddy, don't leave me please daddy don't leave me." I cried all night. My heart was gone. I felt nothing but emptiness and loneliness. The man that I truly loved as my father was now gone. I resigned myself to a little room and for the coming days leading up to the funeral I would hold his picture in my hand, stare at his beauty put it next to my heart and I would drink Harvey's Bristol Cream and I cry myself to sleep clinching his picture. My daddy is gone. In my mind the world is over.

A few days before the funeral I was given instructions by my mother to call Chuck's mother and ask her to get me a suit for the funeral. I followed instructions. It would be her or Clay who I knew would make sure that I looked immaculate for my daddy's funeral. I joyfully picked the phone up and I called my grandma Hattie. I said grandma this is Chip how are you? I said granny which was fine to call her all the other times I went by her house with my daddy and cleaned and painted for her. I said granny would you buy me a suit for daddy's funeral and granny said I ain't buying you nothing. You ain't his son; you are a Trick Baby and she hung up the phone. My heart was shattered. A Trick Baby, what did that mean? Chuck told me he was my daddy chronologically now the reality of it all set in although he had signed the birth certificate; I was not his real son. I was the son of a man whom I still have never met. What she insinuated was I was the child of a whore who had no place in her family. I was a bastard who had no line he could physically trace. I relayed the conversation to my mother what Hattie had said. I wasn't expecting comfort. I knew I would get anger but for what she said, my mother deserved the right to set the record straight. Although she never has clarified who the real father is she gave Grandma Hattie a cussing out that she would never forget.

Life changed quickly for everybody. The welfare system had disappeared. Cars were being repossessed, by his partner houses were being taken, and things had changed literally overnight. I was given one last chance to get to the penthouse to get my belongings. I took advantage of the open door to gather my things. I went into the penthouse and it felt hollow, lifeless. I went to gather my clothes upstairs. I stopped in my daddy's room one last time. The inside thieves had already taken most of his valuables. I saw the robe my daddy had on the morning he sent me out to get my transfer. It was blue and plush and I grabbed it as a memento. I hugged the robe and I smelled his scent and I cried. For whatever reason, I put my hand in the pockets of the robe and to my surprise I found two ounces of cocaine. I quickly gathered my things and I left the house not knowing the value of the drugs I possessed. My life was getting ready to be changed again. Trick baby was about to come up and I would still be next in line for a blessing.

.

Chapter 4 - The Fall

Galatians 6:7 - Be not deceived; God is not mocked: for whatsoever a man soweth, that shall he also reap, KJV

What a spring weekend. The weather was great, my pockets were full my legs were strong, and it was time for a pre-family reunion! My aunt Vickie had just gotten married the night before and all of the family had come together to be a part of this joyous occasion. People, who most of the time couldn't get along, were line dancing and grooving to the latest jams. It's amazing how many people struggle with the Trans Europe Express, but the main thing was we were partying having fun, drinking ourselves into oblivion mixed with an occasional hit of the monkey paw. All things were well. We partied all night into the wee hours of the morning. I remember going to bed at nearly 4:00 am with an excitement that we were getting up going to Cedar Point the amusement park like no other; well at least no other in Ohio. I jumped up at 8:00 am and decided that I needed to go to the Big & Tall Store to get fitted up for this amazing day that was planned for us. I wanted to be a part of the graduating class of 1989 festivities that were taking place at Cedar Point. Even though I needed summer school and a move of God to help me graduate I was proud to be a part of the class of 1989 because we were the preps I was in a makeshift fraternity called the Heights Home Boys which was really a ferocious gang. I mean we were well dressed, articulate to a degree, fighters at the lowest levels, and we had entered into the sexual revolution. We were grown at least in our eyes. I had to be a part of prom weekend even though I didn't go to the prom I still had to be at this legendary weekend that had existed for years. I had to be a part of the tradition, and I had to be fly as much as an oversized big man could be on a Hot spring day. May 30th 1989 will forever be a day that will be marked in my conscience with the scars etched in my body. After shopping for a simple yet classic golf look khaki shorts, a polo shirt, white Nike Cortez's with footies. I had gotten dressed and stopped by to see my stepfather before hitting the highway. I got final approval to drive his 1976 Malibu to Cedar Point. At this time I was having problems with the teenage love of my life, Nikita the Diva. We were having another disappointing round of infighting and she had defiantly decided she wasn't going in protest to my abusive and insensitive ways. It's funny how a wrong decision can turn out to be God's favor sparing you of a tragic moment. I have come to find out what looks bad right then many times turns out for a person's good, for that "No" in defiance literally probably spared Nikita's life. After what seemed like several hours of driving we finally arrived at the Great Cedar Point Amusement Park. Now it was time to have some fun at the park without riding roller coasters.

The park was packed with everyone who considered themselves a legend in their own minds. All of the kids who had become adults too fast were now in the same amusement park. I sensed it wouldn't be long before pandemonium broke out. It was expected anytime you brought people from different neighborhoods together from the Cleveland region. There was going to be fighting or on this day A riot was inevitable. People from the hood and the heights coming together were like mixing acid with honey. It was a hot mess.

It didn't take long, there were fights breaking out all over the park. The Heights Homeboys were fighting the Legends of a 116th. The Legends were trying to hold their own yet they were heavily outnumbered by their suburban foes. One gentleman whom I looked up to greatly because of his style, looks, and cars did his best to hold his own against the pack of human wolves who desired the presidential Rolex that hung from his wrist, but the Rolex he wore was too enticing for the pack of men who began to swing tirelessly at his head until his body slumped where he stood. He unconsciously surrendered the jewels that used to hang from his arm. Fighting was the mantra for the hour, every place you turned there were fights breaking out. It was as though the police had disappeared and anarchy had overcome the pride of Ohio. Cedar Point was due for a catastrophic day that in my mind will never be forgotten.

After the fights had ended we walked the parks for several hours trying to muster up as much fun as we could. We played all of the shooting and water games. I was trying to at least win a big bear to take back home to my teenage love so we could play grown up and make up but I didn't win the big bear but after several hundred dollars of games in the which I could have brought a bear as big as me, I won a small bear with pride. After eating funnel cakes and fresh cut fries it was time to make our exit from the Park life back to the Malibu. I never thought that this day would be the last day that I would enjoy two healthy legs in shorts. The lights were dimming. Darkness had set in. The party was over and it was time to go home. I was exhausted and the drive out of the cramped parking lot seemed to take forever to flow. It felt like traffic was moving in slow motion. I took the opportunity to snuggle in and resign myself to much needed rest; I found the back seat very comfortable. I stretched out as much as I could and created a makeshift bed for myself. I had the perception, as most young people do, that we are immortal, invincible, and we can whip the world. I believed I could tame lions; stay up for days without rest and the laws of nature would somehow conform to my superiority. I never in my wildest dreams thought to ask the driver if he was sleepy. I was only concerned with my own sleep. I remember so clearly the driver making a pit stop for what I believe was ice cream. I remember being asked, "Would you like anything out of the gas station?" With blurry eyes and heavy tiredness and wake up drool on my mouth, I said "no!"

I don't know what time we crashed, I know it was late in the evening because a heavy darkness filled the sky, but I do know that suddenly I was awakened by a pain and a twisting I had never felt in my life and a cry out of my soul as though from the pit of my spirit. I was in the greatest danger I had ever faced in my life! I thought we had hit a land mine because of the fury of the wreck. Boom! The car tumbled down the side of the embankment! I was being tossed like I was a feather pillow that weighed three hundred pounds. I screamed in pain, it felt like my back had broken in half; I will never forget these words that came out of my soul as we tumbled uncontrollably down the side of this cliff.

"Lord help me!" I didn't know the Lord but everything in me knew He was the only one who could help me. The car landed in a ravine of some sort, in utter darkness. I remember laying there as though I was paralyzed, my mind racing about the possibility of death at any moment. I didn't know how to die, I didn't know if I was prepared to die. How do you get right with God? I didn't know a sinner's prayer. I was a sinner who was lost and dead in my sins. The thoughts "I am about to die", engulfed me. I am wounded, my body is in shock. I am surrounded by absolute darkness! As I laid there in a puddle of blood and water, I heard a sound that resembled a drum line! It was my cousin Richard, the driver; he was thrown into the back seat near me! He was unconscious; his heart sounded like it was coming through his chest! I remember trying to be noble. I had assumed that death had its grips on me and either the car was about to blow up or because of my injuries I would be dying at any moment. Therefore, with the little strength that I had, I pushed my cousin out of the car door that was open so that he would be spared. He was between me and the open door, so he fell out of the car to the ground. I could not see him because of the darkness but I could only hear his drum line heart beat doom doom doom. It beat so loudly in the darkness!

Not knowing the severity of my own injuries, I began to rub the leg that I could feel only to have my hand slide inside the interior of my leg! I was wounded as though I had come through an enemy land field. As I lay there, it was as though the sins of living recklessly had finally caught up with me. I had never heard the saying or scripture "you reap what you sow" but I had heard "what goes around comes around."

Just a few days earlier before the accident, as a 17 year old drug dealer who had a few thousand dollars to his name and felt that the world was his, I had cussed my mother out! I told her everything she wasn't! I remember that same day she got arrested for something she had done twenty years earlier and I laughed like it was a joke, but now it wasn't funny as I laid there about to die! I wanted my mother's tender caress; I wanted her to touch me and to tell me it was going to be okay. My mind didn't know how to pray, I didn't know what to say to God. I just laid there waiting for death to grip me. I was afraid; afraid of what I would see when I closed my eyes.

A young lady named Terri whom my cousin (the driver) was dating was in the car during the accident but she had been ejected as the car tumbled down the side of the cliff. I could hear her screaming from the depths of her soul, "Richard! Richard!" It's funny now, but as I laid there I knew she would be OK. Her scream was strong! I selfishly wanted to hear her call my name; I wanted to hear one last person say Chip! No one called! She continued to bellow from her heart for the one she desired to build her life with. Richard! Richard!

Soon I began to hear the pattering of feet coming near the hunk of metal that had been crushed like a coke can under someone's foot! I saw a light beaming; help had arrived! My body was in a state of shock. I was near death and tears were running down my face. The officer came near he looked at me and said "Oh My God." I cried from dehydration I said "Sir please give me some water!" I begged him for water, my body was thirsty! Little did I know but my soul was thirstier; Jesus said "if any man thirst let him come unto me and drink." The officer said "Son I cannot give you water" I cried "please give me water." I cried and begged for water "sir please." He said, "Sir I'm Sorry I cannot give you water!" I have come to find an amazing truth that many times in life the people who look like they should be able to help cannot give you what God has predestined to give you from His very mouth, the bread of life and the water that can fill a thirsty man's soul!

It wasn't long after the officer arrived that a team of emergency workers came on the scene. I will never forget the acts of these men I have never met nor ever thanked personally. This team of men took what is called the “Jaws of life” to pull open this crushed can of a car which caused pain to rip through me as part of my leg was in the metal having been crushed in the fall as it dangled from my body. The men tried to be as gentle as possible getting me out of the car, but the pain I experienced is indescribable. Before they pulled me from the wreckage they cut off every stitch of clothing on my body and then I was placed on a gurney. I was then life-flighted in a medical helicopter which would fly me to the roof of Metro General Hospital in Cleveland Ohio. On the roof of the hospital awaited a team of doctors and nurses who would rush me into an emergency surgery. I was conscious and I remember them asking me if I had been drinking or if I had I been smoking or using drugs. I answered every question and with every question answered I cried for water. I was thirsty like I had never been before. I remember one of the doctors literally screaming at me, “We cannot give you water we are trying to save your life!” Days later I remember waking up for a moment to a male nurse who was inserting medication in me in places I didn't know medicine could go. I was hooked up to every type of device but couldn't speak. So, I groaned as tears ran down my face, I thought that man was the devil himself. The excruciating pain and shame was all too much to bear.

Shackles and tears

I opened my eyes days later again unable to speak but I saw standing before me the most beautiful women in the world; my mother, she was standing in front of me shackled and in county clothes. Tears flooded her face, tears flooded my soul I was so happy in my heart to see my mother. I wanted to tell her that I was sorry; sorry for the way I had treated her. I wanted her to know I was sorry for all of my rebellion and disrespect, but I couldn't speak! My tears said it all, she rubbed me ever so gently and told me, I was going to make it. I sat there and looked at her sorrow and began to understand a mother's love. All of my life I didn't believe that my mother loved me but I was confused about her love. I felt she had abandoned me and my older brother because she had given us away to my grandmother and grandfather. But now I was faced with the truth and I knew she loved me in a way I could never love anyone. The visit was over and she was whisked away by the officers. I laid there unable to speak so I cried myself back to sleep; knowing that my mother loved me.

The news!

I was out of intensive care and had been through weeks of surgery. I was put in a self induced coma and the doctors infused every part of me with pain medicine to help my body deal with the trauma it had suffered.

As I regained consciousness this time I could talk again. My grandmother and aunts were rubbing my head and holding my hands. My grandmother said "baby I have to tell you something. They couldn't save your leg they had to amputate it. Gangrene had set up and the infection was threatening your life." She said "they tried every way possible to allow you to keep your leg and they had to face a harsh reality it was either the leg or your life." My grandmother said when she was faced with the serious possibility of losing me; she made the decision and told them to amputate it. I will never forget telling my grandmother, "Granny you should have let me die, I do not want to live life without a leg!" I was selfish I didn't understand how I could live without a leg, I was 18 years old; I was used to moving and being in the streets, partying! Coming and going when I wanted to. In my mind I was a ghetto legend who happened to look like Al B Sure and Christopher Williams, there was no way in my mind I could make it in life with one leg.

After several more surgeries and several weeks of my amputated leg being in traction, the reality of my new life had settled in and I was ready to return back to the only life I knew; a drug dealer! I called for my closest friends to bring me my pager and to bring me some dope. Right from a hospital bed I began to sell drugs again! I was almost caught several times because I would keep the drugs right in the bed with me not realizing I still had more surgeries. Every time I left the room the nurses had instructions to change my linen, fortunately on this day they didn't change my pillow cases because when I came back from another surgery I awoke with my pillows still filled with my illegal contraband. I had ounces of cocaine laying in my pillow case. I was insane; the nature of death in me was pulling me to be what I was, a sinner. It was pulling me to live from that nature even though I was now crippled physically the sin nature in me still wanted to live a Goliath size life.

I'm in the mood for love

Heavy D was hot during the year of 1989 and I remember listening to his new tape on a recorder someone had given me and I heard the song "I'm in the mood for love." One leg and all I had been afflicted long enough, it was time to go home and all day long I sang this ghetto ballad "I'm in the mood for love." As I was wheeled through the corridors of the hospital, having been there for nearly 7 weeks I changed the tune from heavy D's "I'm in the mood for love" and I began to sing Diana Ross's "I'm Coming Out I want the world to know you got to let me go!" I left the hospital in need of emotional and spiritual healing only to go right back into a life of full blown crime. I was wounded, my leg was amputated and yes many people came to the hospital and prayed for me and with me. I had a school teacher who was also a Reverend from Glenville High School who came up to the hospital with barbequed fried shrimps and other treats daily. He brought me great comfort. I had all of this spiritual support and I had many powerful prayers spoken over my life but I still wasn't changed on the inside. I wasn't born again I was just prayed for. Jesus says it like this in *John 3:3; I say unto thee, except a man is born again, he cannot see the kingdom of God.* I could not see nor understand, nor experience kingdom living because I had not had my heart changed. I was remorseful, I was sorry but I was not born again, my nature on the inside was that of Satan, so as a child of the devil you do as your father does *John 8:44- Ye are of your father the devil, and the lusts of your father ye will do. He was a murderer from the beginning, and abode not in the truth, because there is no truth in him. When he speaketh a lie, he speaketh of his own: for he is a liar, and the father of it.* I was back to living a Lie!.

Chapter 5 - Auntie I'm Home!

I am back on the hilltop at my Auntie Wendy's house. She has a nice two-family on a drug infested street. Belmar wasn't always like that but over a few years what once was very nice suburban living had become a street that could be compared to the building New Jack City was produced in. There were street corner hustlers, mid level pushers, strawberry prostitutes, occasional shootouts and the head cracking of dope fiends on a daily basis for playing dope fiend games like snatching dope and running, paying with short money or not paying for credit they knew they were already on the hook for. Belmar was off the hook, the area had been renamed the hilltop and I'm now called back to live in my aunties house. My leg is gone. Life has changed drastically I cannot walk or run I am in a wheelchair still selling drugs. My left leg is amputated; the leg that I still had is wounded and feels like jelly. I can't use the bathroom on my own. The hospital has sent me home with a special bed and a variety of medical tools. I'll need a urinal and the world famous bed pan. I am physically weak and spiritually lost. My family has to clean my bottom and the bed during episodes of bowel movements. The family took shifts of caring for me nursing me back to health My aunts would come together Wendy, Judy, Michelle. And My Aunt Kim who was and still is an outstanding cook. Kim on occasion would make the best meals ever I will never forget the 2 inch steak she prepared for me. It was juicy, tender and well seasoned. I was getting stronger day by day. The outpouring of support by my family and friends were incredible at the hospital. Dozens if not hundreds came to see me while at my aunt's house. My best friend Jeff was a constant comfort. He lived on the next street and was responsible on occasion for cleaning me and going to physical therapy with me. After a few weeks I would be put in an ambulance daily and taken to physical therapy. I had to learn how to walk but first I had to get strength back into my leg that was also injured. I had been fitted for a prosthetic leg that I hated. It was big, painful and uncomfortable to try on and even more painful to walk on. After a few months of therapy I was stronger, my body was getting stronger and my mind was making the adjustments. I hated not being able to get up and walk when I wanted to but I had made up in my mind I was going to still live an amazing life. I am selling drugs; I'm stacking my chips, I'm moving forward even if it's in a wheelchair.

I had enrolled in the 70001 G.E.D. program. I am going to finish high school. I only needed a few credits to graduate but I took the trainings at the program and I sat for my G.E.D. test. In a wheel chair I got my diploma. I kept moving forward. My time at my Wendy's house had come to an end. My body was going through the horny motions so I had moved back into the house with Nikita and her family who were absolutely wonderful people her mother would serve me tirelessly. Unfortunately Kita and I argued too much and the arguments were becoming more and more physically and verbally abusive. One day after an incredible argument and me rolling out the backdoor screaming obscenities Kita grabbed a knife, having been fed up with my abuse she took matters into her own hands and she stabbed me in the side of my stomach. The wound wasn't deep but it was the beginning of the end. She had already smashed out my truck windows on several occasions and I had smashed in her face frequently. We were crazy teenagers and we went through this violent love triangle over and over again. I moved out I got an apartment on the Lake at the Americana. Life was good. I had gone from getting quarter kilos to being fronted kilos by one of the city's most notorious drug dealers.

In the streets there is a saying amongst drug dealers that you are only as strong as your hook or your drug connection. If you have a weak connection your prices are too high and you can't offer better prices like a Wal-Mart, plus you're limited by the monies you can make. If I only buy ounces it will take me forever but if I'm moving weight I could reach my financial goals much faster. One of the greatest things I thought had occurred while living in Kita's house was meeting a gentleman who used to terrorize the city and was known for destroying night clubs his name was Sean Capone. He was a big black burly man who was known for his violence and a big time drug dealer in my eyes and most of the other hustlers from the Superior neighborhood, and throughout the city. Sean had a daughter by Kita's sister. I happened to be in the right house at the right time. Sean had come to visit his daughter and he saw me sitting in a wheelchair and he began to ask me a series of questions pertaining to what happened to me. I told him my story how I had lost my leg but I quickly changed the conversation of my amputation to focus on his huge supply of cocaine. I informed him I knew somebody who needed some big things. He told me if I could make it happen he would look out for me. I did and he did and we built a short term relationship that was mutually beneficial. His cheap dope allowed me to make more money quicker. Our relationship flourished and we became surface friends; he was on my side. I never played with Sean's money. I had seen him reduce tough men down to groveling sissies. I witnessed him knock a man out who was a known fighting machine in the streets. The gentleman actually had a reputation for being a very tough drug dealer himself but Sean with one punch took all of the legend out of him. Sean was a huge fellow built like a Browns lineman with the temper of a Rottweiler who hadn't eaten in years.

One incident is always etched in my mind as I was rolling into the food court at Severance Mall to grab a bite to eat and to go to the movies. I see Sean heading out while I was going in. He stopped to talk to me in my wheelchair when someone who owed him some money walked up. Within ten seconds a few words were spoken and for the next minute we would be trying to help up a fellow drug dealer off the ground who had been hit one time by this monstrosity of a man. I knew it didn't matter if I was in a wheelchair or not. I knew not to play with this man's money. I could always see him in my mind's eye pushing me out of the wheelchair and me crawling along the ground helplessly taking blows from a man whose anger couldn't be controlled. The relationship didn't last long because his connection ran dry, my money had gotten up and Sean died a violent death. Most people thought he would be gunned down or shot in a police battle but Sean would die riding a motorcycle on the sidewalk and would run dead smack into a regional transit bus. The impact was so great legend has it as Sean's body began to swell as he laid there screaming "get this damn bus off of me." He would be quickly rushed to Huron Road hospital where he would die a short time later.

Life had changed drastically for me. I was balling out of control. I made bundles of cash daily. I was blowing through drugs, my beeper and my cell phone were blowing up I was the new Scarface in the city in my mind!

I was out of Kita's house living on my own selling more dope than Rite Aid. I had a new set of friends who were all hustlers with sex addictions. One of my friends was staying with me. He and his wife were on the brink of divorce. We had daily excursions with all types of women. We had a buddy who was a barber who knew how to make money and he was a part of our inner circle we would connect daily at my apartment on the water. They both had keys. I happened to be out handling some business when Bud decided to stop over and to check me out with one of his beautiful clients. I cannot tell you what he had on his mind for her but I know when I came home I saw a women sitting on my couch that I had to have. She had assumed that the leg that was sitting in the room was some type of statue. It wasn't until I rolled in the house in the wheelchair that she put two and two together and figured out that I was the owner of the leg she had mistaken for a statue. That night we ate Sweetwater's fish and cake. We talked late into the evening. She didn't live in Cleveland; she was still near Columbus, Ohio close to the college she had just graduated from. I got her number and at eighteen had knocked off a beautiful college graduate. I was the man. I had charm. I had money. I was good looking, it didn't matter that the real me, the crazy me would come out over time and cause this woman great pain and heartache. For now my secret was safe. Only I and a few others knew how manipulative, angry, and crazy I really was. For months we courted over the phone and when she came into town and as the feelings grew, I convinced her she needed to move back to Cleveland to be with me. I was coming out of a crazy relationship with a crazy woman about to mess this nice ladies life up trying to have my selfish needs met. Nikita hated the fact I had moved on with someone I deemed to be better than her and I threw it in her face often. One day Nikita fed up with my new life was about to put the icing on the cake. Kita popped up at my bachelors pad breathing fire. She had come to set the record straight, she didn't want me neither did she need me. After a few moments of cussing all I heard was glass shattering. Kita had thrown a brick through the entrance door of the apartment. I was dealing with a woman scorned and she was she about to make me suffer for jumping ship. After all the commotion settled her mother would come and pick her up and that day the icing was put on the cake. We were finished. She was mad and I was glad this part of my insane life was over. I was now redirecting all of this lust and anger to another unsuspecting female.

The apartment I lived in was too wide open. I had brought too many people there to visit including friends and family who were treacherous. Things began to happen. People began to want what I had. I was driving a brand new Acura Legend with ground effect kits sitting on Lorenzo's. I was supplying several brothers with drugs. Jealousy became obvious amongst family and friends. Jealousy is not always people treating you bad. Jealousy is people plotting how they can take what you have. I had a cousin who had his own set of issues. He was angry, hot tempered, violent, and scandalous by nature. He had a takers mentality. He would steal from you without thinking about the relationship or the consequences. I didn't keep a lot of money where I laid my head but I did keep some stacks near me. I knew that if I got busted you never keep your drugs or money in the same place. If they take one, you at least have the other to fall back on. In my mind I had transitioned from a low level thug to a savvy mature criminal. I didn't do business at nineteen like I did when I was sixteen. The game had changed for me. I was moving weight. I wasn't selling fifty dollar packages. I was selling ounces and all parts of the kilogram. If you want it, I had it. You could have whatever you liked! I'm balling and now my family and friends are trying to stick me for my paper.

The safe is empty

I would leave the apartment on this particular day having had a premonition to take all of the money out of the safe and put it in my top dresser drawer under the t-shirts, socks and underwear. I knew everyone knew that I always went to the safe to get money out. It's amazing when you're in the game how everything is game and if you want to last in the game you have to always make adjustments. I had a knowing on the inside to take the money and move it. It wasn't a lot maybe 20 grand, but when the thieves came that hot summer day they got the safe but they didn't get the money. They got a few pieces of jewelry and because they thought the money was where it normally was they didn't ram sack the house they just took the safe. I wish I could have been there when they finally got the safe opened to see their faces. I'm sure it would have fit in a scene from next Friday of the bumbling fools going through all of that trouble to hit a big sting yet to come up empty handed. They got some jewelry but no cash. The money was sitting right in the top drawer under some socks.

I wasn't always so fortunate. I was hit on several occasions always by someone I knew in the game or in life. Most of the time it's not the ones who are on the outside who do the damage many times its those who sit right next to you at the dinner table. Those are the ones who become your worst enemy. Jesus had Judas, David had Absalom, and betrayal has been around since the beginning of time and will be around until time ceases to exist.

I have had a many sad stories about how someone else lost my fortune. I have been awakened in the middle of the night by family telling me the safe house where the majority of my money was stashed had been robbed at gun point. Go figure a place robbed at gun point who the only people who knew that the money was there is family. Money makes people do the strangest most treacherous things you can ever imagine. I came to figure it out the hard way. If I got the money the wrong way it would leave quickly. If it's ill gotten gain it won't stick around. The truth of the matter is even if it sticks and you keep all of the money you have ever made from illegal gains, Jesus says, what does it profit a man to gain the whole world and then to lose his very soul. And what shall a man give God in exchange for his soul for all that we possess in time pales in comparison to what we shall lose if we miss heaven as our final resting place.

The Game is Over!

The early 90's were the beginning of the end for so many. People were buying drugs in every form. For some reason everyone wanted to be high. Dealing drugs got me everything I desired: the finest women, cars, clothes, furniture a false sense of power on the inside. You would have never known it by what I had, but I was wretched, sad, lonely and battling depression; always saying to myself life has to be more than this!

Before salvation came into my life I was chasing the tail of the great dragon. I was led by the wickedness of my heart after feelings that were fleeting and passions that were momentary. I had sold drugs for years. I had slept with some of the most beautiful women in the world and yet I was still unhappy. I gambled for days on end without sleep sometimes winning but most of the time losing thousands of dollar daily. I was chasing a pipe dream. I was looking for satisfaction in drugs, sex, cars, and gambling. I had false power, flunkies and runners. I had employees at the bar, employees at the restaurant. I was opening up beauty salons with the cities top stylist secretly. I was buying apartment buildings and houses. I was hanging out with the biggest drug dealers in the city and yet I was still unhappy. I was thirsty, my spirit was dead. My life was dehydrated. Every time the thrill of sex was over I went into a quiet depression. Every time I won some money at the crap table I asked myself is this it? I was lost and I did not know how to find or fix myself. I knew I was headed nowhere quickly, yet I couldn't stop me. I literally had gambled away a fortune and I was forced to begin with a new drug connection. I hadn't known them long and if my money hadn't begin to dwindle after all the losses I had taken in theft and gambling and if all the bad investments I had made hadn't gone bad, I would have never messed with these guys. But as God would have it, He allowed me to get with a group of guys who were already on fire. The feds were already watching them, their phones were already tapped. I knew they were hot too because every time I would get around them I would feel on the inside like somebody was watching us. I knew it but I kept going further into a no win relationship based upon my need. I was going broke and I needed a lifeline. It's amazing what we do and who we mess with in desperation. My fate was sealed; I didn't know it was the will of God. I hadn't ever heard what the devil meant for evil God would turn it around for your good.

I knew it was a matter of time before the feds came to get me. I had an eerie sense that it was over for me. The game was coming to an end! My connections and his cousin had been busted. I got a call from one of my co-conspirators from jail on purpose he would be wired for sound by the government. He was calling me to make their connection with us sure and recorded. The game was over I understood that clearly the lure of fast cash, fast cars, and fast women blinded me to the truth. The Bible calls it having your conscious seared; my conscious wasn't seared, it was well done, fried extra crispy and burnt!

I was hard beyond flint, my heart was darkened by the forces of evil; the Devil and his crew regulated my life! I woke up every day to evil, trying to fill a void that nothing I could do naturally would fill. I sold drugs, I sometimes used drugs, I gambled, I lied, I played the ladies at least that's what I thought. From what I understand today I was the one getting played but that's another story! I lived a dangerous, promiscuous life that was structured and governed by the kingdom of darkness! I was born and truly shaped in iniquity, it was my nature to live this way, and it was my destiny to fulfill evil! I was raised to believe that this was a natural life for a hood prodigy, I didn't understand that what goes around comes around was really spiritual in nature! In the

Bible it says in *Genesis 8:22 - While the earth remaineth, seedtime and harvest, and cold and heat, and summer and winter, and day and night shall not cease.*

What we sow is what we reap! Meaning the seeds you plant may not grow up today but before long we all reap in life to the degree of what we have planted in life. My seeds had come home to roost! I had been warned by several faithful neighborhood patrons at my makeshift club which was really a small neighborhood bar! Little did I know but in the friendly neighborhood there were people in unmarked cars watching me all along. I remember this one guy who would come to the club and drink like a fish coming into the bar one night saying "Chip you got serious problems on your hands, there's a car parked in the alley that keeps staring over here." I already knew in my heart what was about to happen, I was waiting, biding my time hoping that what I knew was about to happen, wouldn't happen.

I remember the night so clearly that would change my life forever! It was unusually empty in the bar on this night as though the police told all of my customers not to come in because they were coming to get me. People were not coming in at the normal fast pace I was accustomed too. I remember closing up the bar, grabbing my pistol and some drugs and I was about to leave and out of nowhere I had this thought that I needed to ride clean tonight so I went back into the bar and put away the gun and drugs that I had on me. I went to my car got on the highway and as I drove away after a few minutes a young white male wearing an apple hat in the hood trying to look inconspicuous driving an older model type Cutlass or Regal kept acting like he wasn't following me but on the inside I knew he was so I slowed down on the highway and got behind him. I began to follow him playfully, he kept going and I got off at my exit at E.260th Street, only to have the exit barricaded by Police everywhere from every agency!

I remember before I got off the exit I made a phone call to my girlfriend at that time telling her I would not be coming home tonight because I was about to be arrested. As I pulled up to face what awaited me, the police with guns drawn, swarmed my vehicle demanding that I get out of the car. I'll never forget the police officer called me by my formal name; "Kenneth Johnson!" They declared "You are being arrested for conspiracy to distribute drugs!" Life was over as I knew it. I would be charged with conspiracy to distribute drugs. The main evidence would be several phone calls that I said the bad drugs I was sold was coming back like baby milk, In their recordings I simply said to my connect this stuff is like Similac. Those words, and the willingness of the connect and others to testify over the course of a few months, convinced me to plea bargain. Seven plus years was the offer, I needed to take. I will never forget what my attorney told me walking the corridors of his office building. He said if you weren't making fifty grand a day and had put away that money for years your time selling drugs was simply a waste of time. It was a real statement, after paying him and living through my vices I would be going to prison broke.

Chapter 6 - The Power Of Those Words!

I'm losing my mind while waiting to go to jail!

After being let out for a season on bond my life continued to spiral downward very quickly! Even though I had been busted for selling drugs and waiting to begin serving a 7-year prison sentence; I still could not change my insane lifestyle! Every day it was the same recurring nightmare, get up, sell drugs, find a crap game, lose thousands of dollars, go home depressed and then find a woman to try to take away the depression. The cycle never ended and every day I was getting deeper and deeper in debt with the devil, drug dealers and myself. I owed myself change and I couldn't pay the bill. It got so bad I was literally trying to turn myself into prison I would call and ask the B.O.P is my bed ready yet because I was about to sabotage my life further. I was still selling drugs and on this particular day I was riding up and down the streets of East Cleveland when I made a sudden left to go home into Cleveland. I noticed the vice was rolling several cars deep as though they were looking to create trouble for some innocent drug dealer. To my surprise I happened to be the one they were looking for.

It's amazing how God doesn't allow you to totally ruin your life! I heard that a hard head makes for a soft behind. Today I was about to face the music again, the only thing that saved me was God. I had been corner to corner selling drugs. I had collected bundles of money just minutes before the Cleveland vice locked their eyes on my vehicle. It was like they had seen exactly what they had been looking for as the line of cars made a quick u-turn to get behind me. It was during this time I began to stuff down into my fake leg an enormous amount of marijuana. It was a blessing to be handicapped with one leg this day because I used the leg as a drug container. I finally slowed down after my stuffing session and allowed the Vice to run my information. They began to tell me, "we have gotten calls all morning about a person riding up and down every street corner selling drugs and you fit that description." I remember pleading my case that I wasn't a drug dealer and they could search my vehicle but I had already gotten rid of the drugs and my cry was that I was already out of the life. For nearly an hour they searched and went through every compartment in my vehicle never finding not an ounce of drugs and boy were they angry because they knew I was the one who they were looking for.

You know they say God works in mysterious ways! Well God says I know the plans I have for you and they are plans to prosper you and not to harm you Jeremiah 29: 11.

God's plans will come to pass for your life when you are destined to do something for Him. The Bible declares there are many plans in a man's heart but it's the Lords will that will come to pass. God knew I was doing my best to make my life worst and he saw fit in his infinite grace and mercy to spare me from an additional twenty years in prison. Just moments before they had pulled me over I had stopped into the house for a quick pit stop to drop off several thousand dollars and several ounces of crack cocaine. If the police would have pulled me over with those drugs and cash on me, with a current federal case pending in the system,

I would have been a 2 time loser, with the weight I was selling; I would have commanded a mandatory 20 year prison sentence! Thank God for His grace and for His calling, I truly understand when He says many are called but few are chosen. I believe when we get to heaven God will sit many of us down and show us all the times He saved us, spared us, and delivered us from many evil plans of the enemy and the main enemy being the one in-a-me.

WHAT THE DEVIL MEANT FOR EVIL GOD MEANT FOR GOOD.

The Last Drink!

It was over. A street legend in my own mind at least! I had fallen! I was now surrendering to serve 7-years in a federal prison but like any other person who has any street savvy and street credibility it was time for one last party . . . "CHIPS FINAL HOORAH." The sentence was handed down and I knew what I had coming. I was afraid and had not ever gone to prison before. I had a brand new baby girl who I loved dearly, a baby's mama who I had mistreated and I found myself madly in love with her now that I'm going to prison. I was the owner of a makeshift club. I was hurting, lost, and desperate and what does a player do at these times? Does he pray the best he knows how? I remember trying to get religious on God before sentencing. There was a Catholic church down Euclid near the Chardon Road area and I remember going in there and buying me some Holy water taking a drink of it and asking God to take away all of my sins! That night I sincerely got on my knees with the Bible in hand of course I didn't read it but I held it for symbolic purposes and I said, "God please don't let me come out of prison the same way that I am going in." I prayed sincerely from my heart! I said “I'm crazy as hell, I'm violent and I need help!” I said “I don't know how to change but please help me.” Well, that experience lasted for a few moments, as in the next few days I would have my final HOORAH, THE LAST PARTY AT MY CLUB.

I remember so clearly it was jam packed with all the well wishers and hustlers coming to pay their respects and to have a last drink with me THE Legendary CHIPPER! I sat on the bar stool and I looked down the bar stools of people who loved me the best they could, the best they knew how. I saw family, I saw girlfriends, and we all sat there and we drank until we could not drink anymore. The club began to thin out as we approached the 2:00am hour and as people left they began to hug me and cry and tell me how they would miss me. The liquor began to speak through them and through me and before long everyone at the bar was crying and I was a babbling drunk, crying and talking about how I would miss them. Then all of sudden these words echoed the room from my heart, my daughter, my daughter I'm going to miss my baby’s life and I began to wail in front of all these people for over an hour it seemed. It was actually a few minutes but it seemed like an eternity! We wept, we hugged, we said our goodbyes and it was over! That night I tried to make it right with Sonja my baby’s mother and in the morning we would have our last crying sessions as we said goodbye. For her it was good riddance for me it was I wish I would have treated you better the time we had together. It was over and my new life was about to begin as an inmate. I was terrified I did not know what this new world offered yet I had to now face the music of the song I had created.

Next Stop Prison!

I was headed now to my new home at FCI Fort Worth. I was being sent to a medial prison because I thought for some reason it would be easier there for me, so my lawyer asked the courts to allow me to surrender there so that I could be evaluated on what type of prison was best for someone who was an amputee.

Just a quick side bar! You know when I think about how lost I was before I went to prison; it amazes me how my nature wouldn't allow me to stop doing evil! I was in the enemy's clutches. Even when I knew that I was busted, I knew I had a case, I knew that I was going to jail but my nature wouldn't allow me to stop! I gambled more and more and sold more and more drugs! I was addicted to sin and a life of degradation! SICK! The professional gamblers were busting me daily of all that I had and I was trying to save face as I went down a slow death! I had guys who knew I wasn't as slick as I thought I was! They would come to find me daily with buster dice just to take all of my money! For those who don't know what buster dice are; let me explain! They're dice that roll a certain number over and over again. It's having dice that only roll 7 or 11's, and in that case the roller who knows how to work the busters always win because the dice roll in his favor. So I was losing in every way! I was the big drug dealer who was going to prison broke! That's why I understand where some of you are today; your nature will not allow you to change, no matter what! If you dress the part, you look good, you act nice on the inside, you're full of dead men bones and your sin nature is dominating you! I understand so clearly today Jesus talking to

Nicodemus in John 3:7, "Marvel not that I said unto thee, Ye must be Born again."

It's amazing but Jesus said if we are to see the Kingdom we must be born again, if we are going to experience life, not just have an existence but live! Jesus says you must be reborn in your spirit to become a new creation in your heart; if not you can dress up all you want, talk as proper as literacy professors can teach, but you are still dead and lost in your sins and in danger of going to hell! WHY? Because your eternal nature isn't changed! You know you can dress a mule up and bring him to the race track and you can shine him up and make him look good. He can look just like a STALLON HORSE but when you line him up at the gate with other STALLONS and the referee shoots the gun and the gates fling open he will walk around the track, why? Because he wasn't born a STALLON, HE WAS BORN A MULE AND IT'S NOT HIS NATURE TO RUN. In the same breath we may look okay because we look like well to do mankind but in order to be a man like God or a woman like God with the nature of God on the inside of you, you must be born again!

Remember I am headed to the prison FCI Fort Worth to start my-7 year prison sentence. I get off the plane, catch a taxi to the prison but before I go to the prison I decide to do two things. First, go to lunch at Chili's and second, go to a strip club. Remember my nature is at this time is always bent on doing evil. I go to the restaurant and I begin to have a conversation with the male waiter, I get him to open up about the Texas drug climate; I had heard that Texas has some of the cheapest drugs in the country! So I began to inquire about where I can buy cheap drugs on my way to prison. I asked this young man if he could buy some cheap drugs for me and send it back to my city. Now this is on my way to prison my dead spirit is still trying to lead me into dead places. I really needed to be born again. For whatever reason the young man turned down my offer (he was smart) and I got back into my cab that was sitting outside meter running and I asked the cab driver to take me to a strip club where I could see naked women and have a few drinks before I turn myself in to prison to spend the next seven years of my life.

The Twilight Zone!

It's amazing what people will do for money. My cab driver stuck right with me, meter running all the way. He was trying to help me fulfill my last fleshly wishes, going to the strip club! As we arrive at the bar the outer appearance had no allure or mystique to it at all, it was like going into a soup kitchen in the slums of any major city. To my surprise the reality of my need for absolute change became ever so real! As the music began to play the bartender had served me Budweiser after my request for Remy and Heineken had been dismissed! The music blasting, lights dimmed, my last few moments in the free world! The biggest women I had ever seen in my life as strippers came out dancing on top of the bar as passionately as they knew how; my stomach turning, my mind racing out of control. All I could hear within myself is "has your life come to this." It was as though I was in an old remake of The Twilight Zone; all I could hear was the music from the show! I knew that the life as I knew it had come to an end. I was lost out of control on my way to prison and the lust of the flesh and the pride of life had taken its toll on me. The breaking process was being instituted, it was over!

After leaving the strip club FIASCO, I almost ran into the correctional facility, the only hindrance from me running into the prison was I did not know how to run on a prosthetic leg.

Chapter 7 - The Prison

When we asked the court to allow me to surrender at the Federal Prison Hospital we thought we were going to have it so easy. WOW! How my plan backfired! I get inside the prison population, I meet some really nice guys however, I was very naive to the prison hustle but I knew to keep my guards up! I'm now here with the slickest of the slick! I meet Freddy and he helps me out, he goes to commissary with me teaches me a few thing about the institution. I go to my team meeting to talk with the unit managers and counselors and to get my room assignments. Talk about religious preferences which at that time I told the team I was a practicing Jew to the roar of laughter. AT THAT TIME I WAS BEING FUNNY BUT IN GODS EYE HE WAS ALLOWING ME TO PROPHESY PREMATURELY. Remember Paul's words about who is a real Jew; *Romans 2: 28 For he is not a Jew, which is one outwardly; neither is that which is outward in the flesh: 29 But he is a Jew, which is one inwardly; and circumcision is that of the heart, in the spirit, and not in the letter; whose praise is not of men, but of God.*

In the coming days after this comedic team meeting, I was assigned to a room on the first floor, which was supposed to be for my benefit. Now I had been in the prison for a few days and I noticed how the government could care less how sickly a person is if they have committed a crime; they will have to do the time. I met a blind man whom I really enjoyed talking with, he was like an ole school player from the Himalayas; he had stories and game for miles. I also met a gentleman in a wheelchair which is not strange being a prison hospital. But this guy was different he had the biggest arms I had ever seen. He was all upper body, he literally had no legs, No private parts his body consisted of a stomach, arms, a neck and head. , it was the most amazing thing I had ever seen physically. He would tell me later that he was running from the police and they accidentally ran him over (wink wink accidentally). That day it became evident to me that disability or no disability I was going to do all of this time!

My roommate was another story he was in his late fifties, a very thin black man who coughed uncontrollably. His body was full of lesions and sores. I tried to be cordial to say the least but there was something about his breathing and his cough that made me uncomfortable; to say it kindly. I began protesting to my wonderful team unit about removing him from the room or removing me! There was no way we could live in the same room together! It did not seem safe or fair to be subjected to a virus or disease, having made it through the streets of Cleveland to come and die in prison. This didn't sit well with me! After a few days of protest they removed the man from the room. I began a thorough summer cleaning! After a few days news spread that the gentleman had died in the prison hospital of AIDS. He had shared with me that he was sick from using unclean needles. I pray that upon his death he knew Jesus! At that time I neither prayed with him or for him, my nature was as sick as his body was! I was in need of healing!.

Chapter 8 - The Plan of God; Peaches Comes To Town

Prison life at FCI Fort Worth was bad to my flesh. I didn't like the food, I didn't like the staff, especially the correctional officers who ran the kitchen; they were very mean and controlling. The kitchen manager and a lady who acted like she was his wife were always spewing out orders in the most demeaning way. Asking me to do anything at that time was demeaning! I had never really worked for anyone in my life and now I have to take orders from people whose salary I could produce in a week! Me the king, take orders from people whose salaries I made in a week was very difficult. However, the threat of going to solitary confinement for insubordination, or as they said, failure to obey a direct command kept me in line while I went through my evaluation process. I made interesting friends in the kitchen. It was always my desire to befriend the cook because as an inmate he had power that was uncommon for a number. Plus his cooking style resembled more of southern cooking than prison food. He had access to food and cooking equipment which made it so much easier for those who worked in the dining hall. My job at that time was so demeaning at least in my mind! I was being forced to wipe tables and fill napkin holders!

I felt more like a busboy then a Ghetto Legend! But this was all a part of the set-up for the encounter. I was still very immature; I thought as a child, I had not become a man yet! Even though my size was that of Lurch from the Adams Family! Two things prison work did for me. First it started the humbling process, that my number was no different than anyone else's. I was an inmate and I would be an inmate for quite a while and as long as I was in prison, I had better get used to the fact that I would be taking orders and working menial jobs! The second thing was my fine dining experience gave me divine connections. It wasn't that the men who worked in the kitchen were angelic, no not by far. They did use the time to begin to introduce me to the concept of going to church at the prison chapel. At first I was very resistant although I wanted to change I didn't believe my life had now come to this, going to CHURCH!

It's amazing how God can give you exactly what you need even if you don't know you need it. Through a series of unfortunate events at least in my eyes God began to soften my heart to the degree I would listen to the dignitaries in prison ministry. Then on one warm fall night I followed a procession of men into the prison auditorium. Peaches was coming to the prison. I remembered her name "Peaches" because my grandmother in the 70's kept album covers from the worldly artist "Peaches and Herb" which she enjoyed. The men kept calling her Evangelist; I had never heard the word before. I had heard Priest and Reverend but I was interested to know what an Evangelist was. As I settled to prepare for the show, the music began to blare and the men began to stand and people began to clap and her husband began to lead the spiritual concert. They sang/ testified, and then the Evangelist preached. I had never heard a preacher who had moved me, by the end of the service, the Evangelist asked men to come to the altar, to get their hearts right with God. By this time something was happening to my heart, it was fluttering. My heart was pricked and I felt like the Grinch at the end of the movie; my heart had feelings that were warm and gooey. I had tears flooding my soul. I tried to hold back what was in me! A tinkle of warm tears began to cover my face. What happened next still amazes me, my feet begin to follow my heart and I began to walk with an avalanche of men down to the front of this stage where the Evangelist beckoned us to come, to get our hearts right with God. As the music became dull her words became crystal clear! I was a sinner, lost, dead in my sins and the only one who could change me or save me from myself was JESUS! I didn't understand any of it but my heart understood all of it.

I remember standing there at the altar torn between being macho or being broken. I tried so hard to control my tears and to pull myself together but the harder I tried to straighten up the more my heart poured tears from my soul. God had touched me and I didn't know what I mumbled as she prayed with me but that night a seed was planted in me and a yearning to know God was stirred in me. For several months I did nothing to enhance what happened to me. No devotions, no mores songs, no reading of the word; I just lived in a prison both physically and spiritually. Oh yeah I visited the prison chapel on an occasional Sunday but I didn't visit church outside of the devoted Holy Day!

Chapter 9 - It's Time To Move.

My evaluation was over it was recommended by the prison doctors and team leaders that I be transferred to a prison in camp Bradford Pennsylvania. The camps were smaller, easier to get around and I would be closer to home. I was excited to see anyone who knew me from my past, it could have been an arch street revival but to know a familiar face was far too much for my flesh to handle. I remember arriving at the camp after spending several weeks in what the bureau of prison calls transit. Transit is like going through hell to get to purgatory! You sleep on concrete floors if there are no beds available; you eat out of a bag breakfast, lunch and dinner consisting of mainly cold cut sandwiches and rotten apples. The food was not the worst part; it is staying in the cell 23 hours a day waiting to be moved to your final destination. That was the most painful, being restricted doubly is a great term, and it's like being locked up twice.

Transit was over, I had arrived at FPC McKean and what I saw literally blew me away, a prison that didn't have a fence. I saw men running on the track, people playing baseball and young men flexing their crossover skills on the basketball courts. I saw two small buildings that looked like college dormitories that housed three hundred men. I saw people well dressed and manicured, I thought for a moment the bus driver had made a mistake and I was at Penn State University. It didn't take long to be assigned a bed and for me to start asking questions about this place. I dreamed this would be my home for the next 5 plus years. I was blown away by some of the answers I heard from the men at that time; you were allowed to wear clothes that resembled cloths from home. Movements weren't restricted as much, except for count (the guards would literally count the inmates, one by one) and of course you should never cross those imaginary boundaries that exist at federal prison camps. I was overjoyed to say the least. I was close to home, I was already losing massive amounts of weight and with new clothes on I looked like Chico Debarge going to the Mirage. I could not believe how peaceful this place seemed but before long I was shocked back into reality. The correctional officers, not all, but most had a noticeable dislike for the ease of the camp. I remember two officers who reminded me so dearly of Barney Fife from the Andy Griffith Show, but in their mannerisms they acted like the terminator! They were always raiding your locker looking for contraband and they were always spewing out negativity like pythons cornered by hyenas. I did my best to stay clear of confrontation with the Barney Brothers but on occasion my manhood got in the way. I saw myself throwing tantrums toe to toe with these officers that in the end, neither I nor any other number would ever be able to win. It's sad when I think about it now but some of the men who could not resist revenge would do the most terrible acts to make the correctional officers lives miserable. Men would jam the locks to their office. There would be times when an officer would put his hands on the door only to have the knob covered with feces. These men would cause as much havoc as they could without being put out of McKean. The dream of being put out was very easy because people dropped kites at the front office telling of every indiscretion. It was scary to know that even though you were there with 300 inmates and one officer walking the compound most of the time; the front office knew if you sneezed wrong. They knew of every indiscretion taking place, who had gotten drunk, who had gotten into a fight, and who left the prison for a hotel rendezvous. They knew it all, and all of their intelligence came from law abiding reformed inmates.

McKean was too sweet to leave based upon bad behavior. Who would want to leave visits every weekend that allowed you to take a blanket and lay in the grass like you were at a manicured beach? Who would want to leave ordering pizza and subs on the weekend? Who would want to leave the fantasy of feeling free even though you were locked up! McKean the dream had most men not all, on their best prison behavior. I got caught in the trap trying to seem good but I was still no good. My heart was still wicked. Above all things my life at McKean resembled my life in the streets. I was running several different dates on the weekends at the prison. Dressing in Polo, getting fresh haircuts weekly, eating the best, drinking the best and I was locked up! I thought I was doing rather well; at least that's what my flesh told me!

Chapter 10 - Suitcase Willie

Prison had its down days as well, especially when strong men began to cry! I remember having the mindset of "it could never happen to me." I would never be the victim of suitcase Willie. Suitcase Willie is not a figment of men's imagination; he is the epitome of relationship terror. When Suitcase moves into your home it means the relationship is over. Your girl is gone and another man now lives in your house and now drives your car or your ship, if you will! Suitcase Willie is a legend amongst many numbers especially those from the African American community. Most women who decided to move on really didn't need an excuse why they were leaving and going after greener pastures. Most of them had experienced physical and mental abuse. Most had been cheated on repeatedly during the course of the relationship and most were tired but for some odd reason I had it made up in my mind that Suitcase Willie would never come knocking at my door! Then came the visit from hell to cement my place in Suitcase Willie's history!

It was a beautiful summer Saturday and I had gotten my hair cut early that morning and had my outfit creased and ready by the jail cleaners. I was manicured with great expectation of seeing the woman I had so passionately loved now that I was locked up! You know jail will make you think about who's really on your side and who really has your back. I had this wonderful epiphany of how grand my daughter's mother really was, never thinking of how she thought. Only thinking now that I had come to my senses this is really someone I could spend the rest of my life with. Never thinking of all the hell I put her through and all of the sleepless nights she had wondering where I was or who I was with. I never considered all of the violent outbreaks within our private walls of Vietnam that she faced whenever I decided to show up! She never knew who she was going to encounter with me would it be Dr. Jekyll or Mr. Hyde I had Sybil type personalities. It's amazing how selfish a person can be; now that I am locked up, I began to think of every possible way to keep this women whom I had damaged emotionally and spiritually all in the same breath. It's very sad and very serious what jail does to individuals; jail brings out all kinds of emotions. You go through different extremes; it's almost like being bi-polar. As Bobby would say you have incredible highs and terrible lows and now was the visit from hell with me the (the devils little brother) that would cement our relationship in time!

I'm dressed, I'm ready and the entire compound knows that I'm going on another visit I was legendary I had visits during the midweek and on the weekends nobody did it with more frequency and variety. Time was moving quick that morning I expected her to be there on time by 11:00 am, I'm waiting angrily and now its 12 o'clock then 1 pm. By this time I'm completely consumed with anger, and on fire. Breathing like a dragon, and finally walking into a crowded visiting room at 1:15pm! Doesn't she know who I am, how dare she disrespect me to this degree; never in my mind did I think or discern the fact that she has driven 3 hours to get there. I should have known that whatever time she came it was a blessing. However, I was not using common sense, only ghetto behavior worked from where I had come from. I walked into the visiting room completely unappreciative; the first words that come out of my dumb ignorant mouth were “you BLIPPITY BLIP, why did you even come?” I could see instantly that the small flame that was trying to stay lit in her heart, instantly left and the coldness that came over the women who had been scorned for the last hour was unbelievable! However, I begged for forgiveness. She played her hand ever so sweetly, “Oh yeah. I forgive you! I know she didn't mean it”, all the while she preparing herself for the exit, from our last visit! The reality of it was it was time to move on! Suitcase Willie whom she had been contemplating being with was much better than this nut case for sure! The visit was over, The Al Capone wanna be was sent back to his room; I remember looking back knowing on the inside it was over. I tried to look as sad as I could as she waved bye bye and in my heart I knew it was bye, bye for us! This was the day that I lost a major battle as she came to the realization "I am better than this." My girl took her life back and I lost a great friend and part of my daughter's life that I would never regain. I remember walking down the hallway of the administration heading back to the dormitory having my heart in my feet walking through the corridors of hell. I said these words from a bleeding heart “GOD if you're real, I'm crazy as hell, I'm violent and I cannot change myself. If there really is a God please help me. I don't want to be like this anymore.” That day God heard my cry. The next day I reluctantly called home to hear the words from a courageous soldier that had been wounded far too long; “Chip I am moving on with my life.” That day it was over for my relationship with her but God would allow me to be broken, for brokenness in man is the building block for God’s construction team. God uses brokenness to heal the breaches in men’s hearts. I wasn't use to that type of pain and the street terminology is “it's never fun when the rabbit has the gun.” I was reaping what I had sown and now the reality of how fragile the heart and mind are, was before me! I was hurt from hurting someone and hurting myself in the process. I thought my life was over, but God had another plan for her and for me. Today I am grateful for the power this woman had to make a choice to be free and to love again. She moved on and Suitcase Willie was waiting in the background. He showed her a life I could have never given her at the time. He was a stable, hard-working man who had vision and who would never put his hands on her or disrespect her verbally or physically.

God began to work on me in prison! Have you ever heard the term "What the devil meant for evil, God will turn it around for your good." I remember a man named Arturo talking to me with such glowing terms. He spoke with terms I had never heard before and it was intriguing to listen to another man talk with such wisdom. We affectionately called him Art. In his twenties he was serving ten years for a drug conviction and in the process became a very strong Christian. I don't remember his conversion story, I only remember his life. His humility and kindness will forever be etched in my mind. He had a fire for God and he had integrity while most men in prison were trying to come up with schemes to get over. He always walked up right as a man of God full of integrity. I would always quietly creep over to Art's cubicle to hear a word of wisdom or to ask questions about the Lord. He talked with me more from the way he lived than by what he said. Both his life and his words carried weight. It wasn't long before Art had me going to the prison chapel for an inmate-taught Bible study. He really had my engines revving about going to a special service with a church that would come into the prison every so often. I remember going at first because Art had invited me, and I enjoyed what they had to say but for most men including myself the Pittsburgh fellowship brought in ladies that were easy on the eye beautiful to look at. Church would be packed whenever they came. I don't believe many of us really heard the sermons, we may have heard the words but we didn't hear it in our spirits.

At one of the services, the wife of the Pastor got up to pray and I had never heard of the anointing. Now I understand today from my experience at Fort Worth with Evangelist Peaches she was anointed and she preached under an open heaven where God's Glory would meet us. This Pastor's wife prayed with an anointing and this day I experienced something I had never experienced before! I know later in my walk with God I have cried in prayer, sang in prayer, and danced on one leg in prayer but I had never been gutted and purified in prayer like I was when God was forcing me to notice of my need for him through Jesus Christ! I remember when she prayed, her prayers pierced every place of darkness in me. Her prayers flooded light into my soul as though I had been disconnected for years and suddenly the switch was turned on and my soul was reconnected to the source of all power and energy! As she prayed, I did everything to fight off the tears until suddenly a swelling rose up in me and a cry out of the depths of my soul began to bubble up and overtake me.

I remember crying for the entire service as though God was purging me of every hurt I had ever committed. I cried and I cried, I was trying so hard to stop crying but something would not let me go on my terms. He would not let me go until he was finished with me. I remember walking out of the church service feeling as though I had gotten rid of 100 lbs of excess garbage.

God had touched me; I had a sense of longing for more of Him. I began to go to chapel services in the prison. I began to get involved in what God was doing amongst the congregation of inmates! God was wooing me by His love and His presence for a deeper walk with Him. I still was battling fleshly issues. I still had sin in my life but I started going to church just as I was and I started seeking God in the state that I was in, and with the struggles I faced! The struggles were ever so real because I wanted to be cool and to be liked by all of the slick inmates. I still wanted to fit in so I kept going to church and going to the baseball bench for a late night drink. I was struggling with the notion of chasing after women. I wanted God but I still wanted to be a player! As Paul would say in *Romans 7:19: For the good that I would I do not: but the evil which I would not, that I do.*

There are many plans in a man's heart, but it's only Gods will that will come to pass. I walked into the chow hall, a normal routine, for most inmates it's the place where you meet, eat, and make plans for the rest of the day. This day was a little different. A man for whom I had the utmost respect came over and sat at my table and told me about an experience he had just had with God through the hands of Pastor Pat. Pastor Pat was an inmate like us, we thought, but he was very different. He walked around the compound praying under his tongue in a stammer of some sort! He didn't have them all if you will. We thought he was crazy and most men were skeptical about embracing Pat. Especially with the notion that he was sent by God to help us. In our eyes he was a criminal like we were criminals. Pastor or no Pastor he was a number and therefore, guilty of doing something wrong but he always maintained his innocence. To this day I don't know how

Pastor Pat convinced the inmate who sat at my table and told me about his experience with God to go to the prison chapel but what he told me gave me curiosity to find out more about God and Pat. This curiosity allowed me to at least listen to what Pastor Pat had to say. If he could touch this guy he had a great chance of touching me and many other numbers on the compound. My friend told me in glaring terms that Pastor Pat opened up the Bible and began to teach him about the power of the Holy Spirit and at the end of the spiritual lesson through the scriptures, Pastor Pat laid his hands on him and as he described it! A fire came on him and he stood against the wall and he spoke in tongues. Tongues! Holy Spirit! All of these terms were foreign to me. I had barely known who Jesus was; I was like the men who Paul spoke with in Ephesus. I didn't even know there was a Holy Spirit but as fate would have it I met Pastor Pat for myself walking down the corridor of the administration building.

He invited me to a Bible study, and I accepted the invitation. We met at the appointed time and I remember the first lesson was on salvation. He wanted to make sure I was saved and he went over several scriptures that promised me this new life in Christ. For the first time it wasn't just an emotional experience I was beginning to understand the depths of the finished work of the Lord Jesus Christ. I saw the price he had paid, I realized the sacrifice He had made for me and I now understood what I was getting myself into by making Jesus the Lord of my life. It wasn't just a religious act. It was and is the greatest act of the God from eternity in time for a man to give his heart to Jesus and to become born again through Jesus Christ through prayer and faith.

Pastor Pat was a master like I had never seen before in teaching the word and making it applicable to your life. He was a master painter for God and my heart was the canvas he would paint the master piece of a lifetime on. I understood that salvation is far better than misunderstood salvation. When you understand who He is and what He has done it will help you to understand what He requires of you. There have been many preachers come into my life after Pastor Pat who have left and are leaving marks that will never be erased and I thank them publicly. I thank God for using Pastor Pat to help change me in ways untold. What I am about to share with you is the greatest thing that I have ever experienced in life!

Chapter 11 - Heaven Invading Time

The Deliverance

Pastor Pat had given me instructions to go to my room and to meditate on the Acts 2:1-4. He told me to read this out loud over and over again and to get my faith ready to be released. He told me that God was going to fill me with the Holy Spirit right after count. I remember going to my room sitting at my desk reading these scriptures over and over again. The count was over and I hurried to get back to the prison chapel so that I could have this encounter with God, the one that Pastor Pat promised! I would only have to get there and another lesson had been prepared. He kept telling me faith cometh by hearing and hearing by the word of God. So he sat me down and for thirty minutes which seemed like eternity, he walked me through all of the scriptures that promised me this gift of the Holy Spirit. Acts Chapter 1 and 2, then 3, 1st Corinthians Chapter 13 and 14 and Romans Chapter 8 and then we came backwards and stopped at Luke Chapter 11. I saw how much more my heavenly Father shall give the Holy Spirit to them that ask Him.

I remember the lesson over and over, my faith was ready but no one expected what was about to occur. Not the preacher, nor the men in the room including me. Pastor Pat asked me to stand and to say a simple confession of faith, "I thank you Lord that I'm filled with the Holy Spirit and I will begin to speak with other tongues as the Spirit gives utterance." Pastor Pat said "say it three times and on the third time I'm going to lay my hands upon you as a point of contact. When I lay my hands upon you open up your mouth and you will begin to speak in a language you have never spoken in before. As the Bible evidenced that you are filled with the Spirit of God." I was like okayyyyy! I'm going with the flow. I get to my last "I thank you Lord that I'm filled with the Holy Spirit and I begin to speak in other tongues as the Spirit gives me utterance." My heart is racing my mind is trying to figure out all of what's happening and how God is going to fill me with Himself. I remember trying to move my lips and to say a few words to release my faith but before I could muster up anything to say, Pastor Pat laid his hands upon me. It was as though a portal from heaven was opened and a power struck my spirit. It was as though three million volts of energy was flowing into me. I remember trying to move and I couldn't, it was as though I was paralyzed in the spirit. I remember shaking violently as an eruption came from me and God pulled out of me demons that were inside and they came rushing out screaming and hollering.

I could hear the men in the room with my natural ear, they were screaming at the preacher and he was yelling to them "he has demons and they're coming out." After this powerful electrifying deliverance, immediately upon the demons departure, God began to fill me with his precious Holy Spirit and for nearly two hours I sang with the chorus of heaven. I sang in a language I had never spoken in before in my life. It was not a language men could teach me but for nearly two hours with my hands stuck in the air, I sang the most beautiful songs. Songs never taught or learned by man. I met GOD ALMIGHTY THAT DAY FOR MYSELF, HE WAS NO LONGER EVERYONE ELSE'S GOD, HE WAS MY GOD TOO!

I was truly born again! I went from being a criminal to a Christian that day. From singing songs of the world to singing the songs of Zion! I went from being a hellion to being a worshipper. I will always be eternally grateful to God for sending me to prison and for sending Pastor Pat into my life to help usher me into my purpose. My walk to the cubicle that night was like Peter walking on water. I was spellbound in the spirit totally amazed and shocked that the God who ruled the heavens, the earth and all mankind was living inside of me. The God that demons bowed down too was residing in me! God had zeroed in on a felon in a prison chapel in a city I had never heard of in my life called Bradford, McKean. God had me on His mind, He was thinking about me. I understood now when He tells *Jeremiah 1:5 before I formed thee in the belly I knew thee; and before thou camest forth out of the womb I sanctified thee, and I ordained thee a prophet unto the nations.* I finally arrived back into my room, coming through a congregation of men who were sitting at the stairs near my room. I'm walking on water literally it felt like I was floating, I was on a cloud and I can remember John and Joe looking strangely at me and saying "what's wrong with you?" Walking ever so lightly, as I walked with my heavenly stride, without stopping and going right through them I said "I just met Jesus." When I arrived at my room I sat there at my bed still in utter amazement. A famished feeling hit my soul; I went to the locker and looked for the meal of the hour fit for a King on this night. I made myself some delicious peanut butter and jelly sandwiches. I remember sitting at the edge of my bed asking myself questions, I asked "are you still in there?" Then I started speaking in tongues again! I remember finishing off the sandwiches and lying on my side with tears flowing down my face. I prayed myself to sleep that night, praying in the Holy Ghost! I had never slept so lightly! I didn't wake up like usual in the middle of the night having muscle spasms, or having foot and leg cramps. The pain was gone the heavy burden was lifted; the stone was rolled away from my heart. I was brand new and when I awoke in the morning it wasn't to Hustler magazines and shame. I woke up full of the Holy Spirit of Almighty God! I was changed on the inside. I feel His presence right now! Forgive me as I preach to myself, the Lord changed me, the Lord has delivered me, the Lord is so wonderfully real to me. No more confusion about Islam! Now I knew that Jesus was the way the truth and the life and I had come to meet my Father! I was a son of Almighty God, I had love in my heart and I had joy that the world didn't give and the world couldn't take it away! I was redeemed, Blood brought and Blood washed! IF I COULD HAVE SANG IN MY NATURAL LANGUAGE THEN THE SONG WOULD HAVE BEEN "CHANGED, CHANGED, I KNOW IVE BEEN CHANGED BY THE POWER OF THE HOLY SPIRIT GOD IS REAL AND THERE IS NO PLACE FOR ANOTHER I HAVE BEEN CHANGED THROUGH THE POWER OF JESUS NAME HALLELUJAH".

Chapter 12 - Trying To Get Back

Matthew 12:43-44 - When the unclean spirit is gone out of a man, he walketh through dry places, seeking rest, and findeth none. Then he saith, I will return into my house

After heaven had touched the earth, after God had invaded time from eternity for my life, I had a strong desire to know the One who had arrested me by His spirit. So I began to read the Bible having no clue where to start, I started reading the Old Testament. I found the stories fascinating. The things God had done for His people. I was at a place in my life that whatever the Bible said was absolutely true. It could have said that Jonah swallowed the whale and I would have believed it! If Pentecost was real everything else in the book was real. If God was still a deliverer and he still cast out devils He was still able to control the affairs of men. I devoured the Old Testament within a week. I had read the entire Old Testament chapter after chapter, tirelessly until it brought me to the door steps of the New Testament. With my Bible reading, I had a longing to stay on my face seeking God in prayer, I would literally pray for hours every day. I was either praying or I was reading I tried to live a balanced life. Workout a little, play a little ping pong which was my favorite sport of choice. Whatever I did, the moment I felt I had played too long, I either ran to the chapel to pray or I went to my room to seek His face; I wanted to know God in an intimate way. I wanted to be close to His presence and I wanted to hear His voice more clearly than the voice of the world. I wanted to hear God more clearly than the voice of people; I wanted to know God from the depths of my soul. My prayer life brought great attention to the Kingdom from men and demons.

My cubicle was right next to the laundry room. Having no door or any real privacy anyone who came to the laundry room would stand and stare in amazement as I prayed in the Holy Spirit for hours. I would have Arabs and people of other ethnicity's come to me after my prayer excursions and say things like "I didn't know you spoke in all those languages." It was as though God was speaking through me to speak to them. I was praying in the tongues of men and of angels. My prayer life transcended that of being just a black man praying in his native tongue to a fire-baptized believer praying the languages of men and that of angels. I remember praying so passionately at the side of my bed this particular time in my heart I heard the lord say "look up!" To my utter surprise I did not see natural people staring at me but for a brief moment in the spirit I saw what looked like a black midst hovering over me. The mist had a form like a man and it was staring at me as I prayed. When I looked up in the spirit, I was startled and the form disappeared. I understand today that when an unclean spirit leaves a man he tries to come back to his house, and when he comes and notices that the house is empty and clean he then goes and finds more spirits even more wicked than himself and tries to move back in and to make the latter state of the man worst than the first.

I see this as one of the major problems in our Christianity today; it's not that God didn't do a cleansing work, the problem lies after being saved, delivered, and filled with the precious Holy Spirit many people fail to fill their houses with the furniture of the kingdom. The devil recognizes people who have a prayer life. He can look into their spirit and see if they have power or if they don't have power. This is why Jude says in *Jude verse 20, But ye, beloved, building up yourselves on your most holy faith, praying in the Holy Ghost our spirit becomes charged with the glory and power of God as you stay in the spirit praying you stay connected to God.* After salvation many people become worse if they don't stay connected to their source. I see it on a daily basis. People come to the altar to be saved and to be filled with the Holy Spirit and God does His part but they don't do their part. They never come back for discipleship classes, they never learn how to pray and seek the face of God praying to get results and many of these wonderful saints become worse as Christians than they were without God. The devil comes in through deception and builds strong holds in their minds which affect their quality of living. I wish that as a pastor the moment that people say yes to Jesus, we could just take the people and place them right into basic training for the next 6 weeks. In basic training we would teach people throughout the entire course of a day how to pray, how to worship, how to study their word and how to legislate according to the Word of God. We would teach them how to fight in the Spirit and become soldiers in the army of the Lord. We need good soldiers in the army who know how to fight this good fight of faith. I want to encourage you to chase after God; run after His will for your life. The only way you can know His will is by knowing His word and learning to follow the voice of the Holy Spirit.

Nothing else in life is more important than having a strong vibrant relationship with God. Every believer should be strong in the Lord, and in the power of His might.

What the devil meant for evil God will turn it around for your good!

Life was different for me now at the camp, I was saved and I was committed to God and on fire. I had given up prison dating or if I was to be honest many of the ladies that used to come and see me had given up on the three hour ride. Many people had given up accepting my calls and sending money orders. They had served their purpose in my life. It was now time for God to be my comfort and my shield and exceeding great reward. My relationship with God began to isolate many relationships that I had on the compound with many of my friends; a lot of which were Muslims, most of them still enjoyed sin.

I struggled with being labeled as the square, but at the end of the day I had made up in my mind. I would rather live for God than to be approved by men. I began to get on people's nerves inside of the prison. I became a Holy Roller of sorts; my conversation always came back to Jesus and getting the person to make a decision to give his heart to the Lord. I became an avid soul winner; God was anointing me to win souls.

I had a passion to pray with and for people, it didn't matter if you liked me or didn't like me I prayed to God and asked for open doors into the hearts of the men on the compound. On many occasions God gave me favor to win souls to His Kingdom. As my popularity waned as the prison player it became more evident to people that my life was being cemented in Christ. I began to be very active in the prison ministry helping to lead services and to orchestrate times of prayer with the men. God was opening up my heart to do more for Him. I remember asking many of the mature saints in the prison "How do you know when God is calling you to ministry?" I got a variety of answers, but the one that stuck with me most was "you just know on the inside." I started seeking God about if He was calling me to ministry. I had this passion to serve Him and to do His will, and I just had a Soul stirring on the inside that I had been called to ministry.

I found myself in the Word and asking repeatedly, "God are you calling me? God are you calling me?" I am sure I sounded like a broken record to God, but in His love He saw fit to confirm the calling through His word. I was studying intensely and for some odd reason my studies led me to a scripture found in 1st Timothy 1: 12-15

> 12 And I thank Christ Jesus our Lord, who hath enabled me, for that he counted me faithful, putting me into the ministry;
> 13 Who was before a blasphemer and a persecutor and injurious: but I obtained mercy because I did it ignorantly in unbelief.
> 14 And the grace of our Lord was exceeding abundant with faith and love which is in Christ Jesus.
> 15 This is a faithful saying, and worthy of all acceptation, that Christ Jesus came into the world to save sinners; of whom I am chief.

When I read this passage of scripture, every bell went off on the inside of me, and I knew God was speaking to me and confirming my call through this passage of scripture. It was literally like God equated this text to my life. I had found myself in scripture and the words began to jump off the pages and I began to shout, “I see it Lord I understand what you're saying.” God was saying He was counting me faithful to this ministry in spite of all the terrible things I did in my past. The thing that cemented it in my heart was this passage *1st Tim 1:15; This is a faithful saying, and worthy of all acceptation, that Christ Jesus came into the world to save sinners; of whom I am chief.*

God had made it ever so plain that He takes people who have storied pasts, people that were the worst of the worst and He uses them for His Glory. I fit the bill perfectly. I was that sinner who had done it all. In my eyes and in the eyes of many people in the world, I was one of the worst sinners who had ever existed. My nickname was the Chief Sinner, but God loves taking the gutter most and making them the uttermost.

I was called by God and I came to find out through great adversity that the calling comes with great pain, many trials and much affliction. I was doing my best to be a super saint trying to live for the Lord. I had given up chasing women from a prison cell, drinking liquor illegally but my mind was still going through a transformation. I hadn't arrived in every area. I was trying to be humble, but my mind equated humility with being a straight lame. I still had a tough exterior to deal with on a daily basis; crucifying the flesh was no easy matter. I didn't care how saved I was there wasn't going to ever be a disrespecting of my manhood. Many a man tried me while saved, and I had to go back later and repent. I remember an incident where a gentleman was running rough shod over the telephone. He must have thought it was exclusively his to the degree a small ruckus got started. I tried to intervene and answer a response to who was next over the telephone only to have telephone lover try to check me in the most demeaning way. I had one of those "all of a sudden moments" where I forgot I was saved and before I knew it I had hit the man upside the head, knocked him silly nearly unconscious while he held the phone. Later grief and remorse over took me; as much as I tried to apologize, the young man had death on his mind. And I was the prime candidate to be stuck like a hog in Arkansas being prepared to be sold on the open market. As I walked outside of the building I was ambushed by a man wielding a sharp object, he was trying to stick me. Like fighting in the West Side Story, he would lunge and I would do my best to move out of the way. The difficulty came in trying to move as fast as he did having a prosthetic leg. I had to fight a strategic fight being at a disadvantage on one leg so he lunged and he missed but grazed me nearly puncturing my side stomach wall. I grabbed him with all the life and strength I could muster slamming him to the ground, but in the process my leg was disengaged from its suction fit. I'm holding him tightly so that he cannot swing nor stab me when all of a sudden a hometown hero named Sam who on this night looked like an angel came from out of the building swinging first asking questions later. He knocked the gentleman off of me and the young man fled. My friends picked me up off the ground my wound being minimal, but my heart grieved to the maximum! I was a Christian man called by God in a fist fight over a telephone. I realized then that there truly is always a war going on in me, and I was going to have to learn to kill my flesh on a daily basis. Peter says it's like this 1 Peter 2:11;

11 Dearly beloved, I beseech you as strangers and pilgrims abstain from fleshly lusts, which war against the soul;

Paul says it this way 1 Corinthians 9:27; But I keep under my body, and bring it into subjection: lest that by any means, when I have preached to others, I myself should be a castaway.

I had to learn to live from the inside out. I knew that my spirit had to learn to dominate my flesh. If not, I knew that I was going to get myself into a world of trouble. The day came when my prosthetic leg was broken while walking around the compound. On crutches, the people who ran the kitchen gave me orders that whenever I didn't have my leg on to come to the front of the line where they in turn would have someone to help me carry my tray of food to a table. I was following orders fully. The line wasn't that long but I decided to make my way to the front to comply with what I had been instructed to do. I noticed that one of the Barney brothers correctional officers was sitting in the corridor paying close attention to the line leading into the chow hall. As I made my move to the front, the officer quickly asked me what was I doing cutting into the front of the line. I explained to him what I was instructed to do by the officers who ran the chow hall and he informed me in the nastiest terms that he could care less what they said, "I'm telling you to get to the end of the line." I kept saying but sir and he kept ranting and raving about what he said and angrily I got into the line as he stared me down shaking his head at me as if to say," you Jigga Boo, don't you know who has the power." This scenario was playing out in my mind and I tried to gather my composure but the intimidation pursued. He kept staring at me and where I'm from I was being punked! I was taking it like a man, I thought but I made the mistake of asking him why he was doing me like this only to hear him to tell a grown man to shut up and to get to the end of the line. I snapped on crutches, I threw them to the ground and I gave him the tongue lashing of the century with a verbal threat of what I would do to his scrawny little behind. Within moments it was like a made for movie metaphor coming to pass! CLINK, CLINK, I was locked up on crutches, sent to the inner prison called the hole. I was placed in solitary confinement for nearly 60 days. I looked defeated in the natural eye, but later God would remind me of my prayers before I got sent to the hole. I was praying to God to get me out of the backwoods of Pennsylvania send me to a place that has real R&B radio stations, put me around some guards who look like me. I didn't realize that answered prayer sometimes comes through painful situations. In any event my first night in the hole was very interesting. A young man I had become good friends with was to be my bunky for only one night. He was locked up for deciding to leave the compound without permission for a quick rendezvous with his girl at the local hotel; only to be caught before he was ever to make it off the premises. What's funny about this situation is before he attempted to leave, he came down to speak with me in his black sweat suit looking like a cat burglar in a Hollywood movie. I told him emphatically, "don't Go!" I let him know I had inside information that the officers would be out in the woods waiting for brothers attempting to make their move to the hotel. Like most men who are led by their lower extremities, he went anyway only to be trapped like a tiger hunted in the jungles of Africa. For months I had witnessed to this young man about making Jesus Lord of his life. He, in turn would try to witness to me about the benefits of being in the Nation of Islam. We both kept coming to the place of a stalemate. At the time neither of us made much ground in our converting each other to our respected religions. But on this night in the inner prison my friend had a desire to know more about Jesus! That night we sat up and talked about the word of God! God was using our tragedy for His Glory; before we fell asleep he had given his heart to Jesus! Only to be awakened a few moments later with the instructions to pack up he was being shipped out. God had gotten the Glory in the last hour of our time together; he brought another soul into His Kingdom and this you man is actually a member of my church today. God would use my cell for the next two months as a sanctuary to win multiple souls into His kingdom and to begin my training as a pulpit preacher.

An older gentleman in his forties was sent from the camp to the hole. I remembered him for being rather silly on the compound, kind of old school with bad jokes. He could lighten up a room with his charismatic personality, now he was my cell mate; in the inner prison we were bunky's. I remembered asking old school if he would critique me on my first sermon. I took the bible and I read from this text out loud as confident as I could *Psalms 27:13 I had fainted, unless I had believed to see the goodness of the LORD in the land of the living.*

I begin to minister to my large and enthusiastic crowd in my mind. I was preaching the gospel only to notice that my one-member congregation had tears running down his face. The word of God and the anointing working through me had pierced his heart. That night he gave his life to Jesus. The hole had become a rest haven for the hurting. God used that place to perfect me as a disciple and to hone my skills as a soul winner. The space was used to reach men who in a pubic atmosphere on the compound would have never come to the prison chapel to hear about the finished work of Jesus. Our God is an awesome God!

My time was up in solitary confinement. Only I wouldn't be going back to the camp I was being shipped back behind the walls on a disciplinary transfer. The unit team was teaching me a lesson and sending a lesson to the other numbers that insubordination would not be tolerated. My new temporary home would be at FCI Petersburg in Petersburg, Virginia. The transit to make it there was painful as you are bound waist hands and for those with normal legs ankle chains are used. We took a federal prison plane that Wesley Snipes and Tyrese could have made their next block buster in. Men corralled like cattle destitute, broken, and angry and at the end of the day there was nothing you could do about it especially seeing that every officer was armed and dangerous. When I reflect back to the trip to Petersburg the plane flight wasn't as bad as the bus ride after we got off the plane. The bus was old, stinky, cramped and hot. The bathroom was big enough for Mini-me from Austin Powers, so the men did their best to hold off trying to go to the rest room bound and restricted by shackles. They fed us bag lunches consisting of bologna on bread and half rotten apples and a juice comparable to a little hug. It was torturous to say the least, but we made it to the prison FCI Petersburg.

I noticed immediately that people who looked like me were running the prison. I was shocked to say the least, and then came the processing of the herd. They placed us in a holding area while we were assigned beds on the compound. I'll never forget the goodness of God while waiting to be assigned a room. It's nearly midnight; men are going up to their rooms. I was told I would not be able to leave yet because they were trying to get me my own room. "My own room" I shouted, yes your own room with a door and you will be by yourself! I thought I had died for a moment and had gone to heaven. I was use to open dorms, no rooms and a whole lot of noise. My mind was replaying what had happened where I had come from and what I was hearing now. I was in awe of the favor of God! I felt like Joseph in the prison with favor on my life. I remember they put me into my temporary room in the holding area and a young black high-energy officer came over and began to talk with me. I was tired and I was hungry and he asked me if I would you like something to eat. It was midnight and I'm like "please yes!"

He came back with two trays filled with cheeseburgers and tater tots! I have hit the jackpot. The officer stands at the door of the cell and he begins to share with me that he is a minister spirit filled fire baptized, a tongue-talking believer! We are at the door of the cell shouting! I'm blown away by what I feel and what I'm hearing and it doesn't hurt that I'm full of burgers and tater tots. God is an awesome God! The next day I'm placed in my private sanctuary. I meet with my unit counselor he goes over my file and tells me the previous counselor has taken away all of my privileges. They have sent a memo saying my commissary and all of my belongings are to be restricted for 90 days. I'll never forget what this counselor told me. He said "this will not be honored here you have suffered enough!" All of your belongings and privileges will be restored today. I was sitting there in disbelief armed with a second chance at prison ministry. I got my belongings went to the commissary, turned on the radio and to my utter amazement; I had access to several black radio stations, Gospel music and Christian teaching radio. God had answered my prayers and everything the devil threw at me to destroy me and to break my confidence in Christ, God turned it around for my good! Whether it was being thrown in the hole or being transferred to another prison; the devil's plan didn't work! The counselor's recommendation for more punishment was even blocked! God turned every evil situation around for good. Glory be to His Holy Name!

Chapter 13 - Nick At Night

John 7:50; Nicodemus saith unto them, (he that came to Jesus by night, being one of them,)

FCI Petersburg was like night and day from McKean the Dream. This was a prison with men who were not going to the office to tell about every little thing that was happening on the compound. This place had its own form of justice and it always consisted of hurting you first and asking questions later. I saw men who had homemade knives fit for a shogun warrior and who would use them in a moments time without reservation. I noticed that the Washington DC guys drank from a different lake than most of the men in prison. They had a hardness that made my tough Cleveland self look like Jay Jay from Good Times.

I adapted quickly to my new environment seeing I had my own room and I wasn't given a job because of my disability. At this prison I spent a lot of time praying and practicing the presence of God in my life. When I say practice, it was spiritual training for me, it was learning to create an atmosphere through prayer, praise and worship that would cause Heaven's Glory to come and rest on me. I saw that the more I exalted God's name and told Him of His power and rehearsed His past victories in my life, the more of His tangible anointing was released. I remember praying in my room and worshiping God in the spirit and all of a sudden I began to pray in different tongues. A song broke out from my spirit and it was as though an unseen force took me on one leg and I began to praise dance in the spirit as though I had trained with a ballet company from Harlem. God's presence filled my room and I danced on one leg for what seemed like hours in the presence of Almighty God. I remember when the anointing lifted I just passed out drenched in the Glory of God. I rested that afternoon in a peace that passes all understanding. God's presence became more and more real to me, the more time I spent with Him the more He charged my spirit and whispered in my ear. I have come to this simple understanding: the more time I seek Him early He will be found. *Proverbs 8:17; I love them that love me; and those that seek me early shall find me.*

God has always desired to have an intimate relationship with His people. He wanted to be Israel's King and God, but they had a desire for someone they could see and feel and God gave them exactly that in Saul. Someone they could see and feel who ruled over them with a hard hand! Was that Gods best? No, was it what the people desired? Yes! God desires to be the God of the church and the head of the body of Christ individually and corporately.

> 2nd Corinthians 6:16-18; And what agreement hath the temple of God with idols? For ye are the temple of the living God; as God hath said, I will dwell in them, and walk in them; and I will be their God, and they shall be my people.
> 17 Wherefore come out from among them, and be ye separate, saith the Lord, and touch not the unclean thing; and I will receive you,
> 18 And will be a Father unto you, and ye shall be my sons and daughters, saith the Lord Almighty.

God wants us to have a relationship with Him. Many times we chase after personalities and formulas but never being re-formed by the Rock and matured by His spirit. We often choose to be cut out and stamped by the hands of men. It's really not funny! We would have a greater quality of life if we learn to hear the voice of God and learn to make decisions based on His Word. We have to follow God with all of our hearts, mind and soul not living as compartmentalized Christians on Sundays and midweek services. Prison life is like free life. Every individual has to make up in his mind whether he's going to allow prison to do him or if he is going to live his life! You have to decide free or locked up are you going to be positive or negative! You have to decide when life serves you lemons you have to turn it into lemonade; you have to make choices on a daily basis. In prison I saw a lot of good men make bad choices and I saw bad men who had no desire to change make worse choices.

God Always Scores The Touch Down

Isaiah 61; *The Spirit of the Lord GOD is upon me; because the LORD hath anointed me to preach good tidings unto the meek; he hath sent me to bind up the brokenhearted, to proclaim liberty to the captives, and the opening of the prison to them that are bound;*

I had been standing on this scripture for over a year! Confessing it over and over again, that I was getting out of prison early. I would declare He has opened the prison door to me who is bound. I didn't realize answered prayer meant I was going to be shipped from McKean the Dream to being locked up in solitary confinement for nearly two months and shipped off to a prison in Petersburg, Virginia! But as I look back, I now realize that the wisdom of God was in operation. There was no way the unit team and drug counselors were going to make the recommendation for me to enter in the drug abuse program, they had it out for me. And it was my entire fault. Before I got saved I had lived a life in prison on the edge and now the very people I had outsmarted, I needed! I needed them to make a recommendation in order for me to enter a program that would take nearly 18 months off of my sentence and it wasn't happening!

I had been turned down on several occasions for the program and every time they turned me down I would go back to God and say, "but you said that you would open the prison doors to them that are bound." I kept reminding God of what He said according to His word.

Isaiah 43:26 Put Me in remembrance [remind me of your merits]; let us plead and argue together. Set forth your case, that you may be justified (proved right)

So daily I reminded Him of all the things I could do for him, free! I argued the merits of my case daily with God, I wanted to be free. And freedom came with a great price tag. I remember going into the psychologist office who determines if you qualify for the program or not and he looks at my file and tells me "I'm sorry Mr. Johnson but you don't qualify." I go to my room visibly shaken. I was stunned. I knew on the inside this was my breakthrough only to hear the words again you don't qualify. I had a decision to make would I accept his no as the final answer or would I go back to God and declare that I believe His report. Fortunately for me I had just read a faith building article by Kenneth Hagin that said "God always Scores the Touchdown!" I remember lifting up my voice unto the Lord and I began to declare that He was greater than Troy Aikman, Michael Irvin and Emmitt Smith and that He always scores when we need him. I worshipped the Lord on that day and the next day. Then one day I got a call from the secretary of the unit team and she had made some calls on my behalf to verify something that was in my file. She then forwarded this newly researched information to the prison psychologist who promptly called me back to his office and he uttered these words "I don't know why I'm giving you this program but you now qualify!" What he didn't know was that I was qualified before; he just wasn't in tune with the same frequency I was listening too from heaven. With a loud shout "Hallelujah" and a befuddled look from the shrink I walked out of there leaping shouting and dancing! God was opening the prison doors to them that were bound the Word of God and prayer was working on my behalf.

I stayed at FCI Petersburg for several months before my departure to the drug program which would be at FCI Milan. I was excited to know that Milan had a huge reputation for having the best prison ministry in the system. They were famous for their Monday night services. While waiting to be transferred to Milan, I witnessed daily and led many people to the Lord. I prayed for many men in my room, they would come knocking at midnight like Nicodemus, afraid to be seen with someone who was considered a Holy Roller. But they knew that God had His personal hand on my life. One incident that sticks out in my mind is a young man from New York who lived on my floor. He would always come down to speak with me. He asked me questions about the Lord. Well on this occasion he found himself and a prison nurse in a world of trouble! They had become forbidden lovers to the degree they both became so relaxed in their illegal love that they got caught. He was being shipped out the next day and came to say his goodbyes and get prayer for the road. I sat him down fascinated to hear his story. I had never met another number who actually dated a prison employee! He told me how it happened and now he was being sent off to a remote prison much farther away from New York than he would like to be. I prayed for the man of the hour and I prayed so hard for him the anointing of God fell on him sitting on my steel toilet. I lead him in the sinner's prayer and he gave his life to Jesus.

I then with a Holy Boldness, told him to lift up his hands and asked God to fill him with his precious Holy Spirit. He willfully obliged and God graciously met him right there sitting on a prison toilet, God filled him with the Holy Spirit and he began to speak fluently in another tongue. I sat there amazed at the Word of Faith and its Power! He didn't need anyone to lay hands on him. All he needed was a release of faith from a believing heart and a confessing mouth. I would employ this new found revelation at every prayer opportunity God would give me. I led many men in that prison to experience the fullness of the Holy Spirit not by the laying on of hands but by the releasing of faith through the confessing mouth and the believing heart! Our God is bigger than our hands! Our God needs only a person who would dare to believe and activate His word! Our God is an awesome God!

Chapter 14 - Milan, The Prison Like No Other!

Before I could get unpacked neatly, I was headed to the chapel area of Milan. I heard they were having Bible study that night and I anxiously arrived in a classroom full of men being taught the word of God by another number. I didn't have a problem with him being an inmate I had a problem with his teaching. He was a word of faith hater, a Pentecostal basher he hated anyone who preached about prosperity or the Holy Spirit! Now here I come, a man of faith full of power and the Holy Ghost! I was coming to be fed the bread of life from heaven. The only problem was that his bread was stale and full of the traditions of men which make the word of God of no effect. I tried to grit and grin through one of the most horrific Bible studies I had ever attended. Then he started using names of the preachers he couldn't stand he didn't like Copeland or Dollar and he despised Pastor Hagin. I found myself in utter shock. I thought love never failed. I didn't know that in this Christian Army we try to wound and kill each other. I felt my righteous indignation boil to the point that I asked him who made you judge and jury! Who art thou that you should judge another man servant. I then gave him a two minute lashing on his limited revelation of the truth, and his disregard for following the commandments of Love. Love works no ill to its neighbor. I remember the eyes of the congregation being fixed looking at me as though I had challenged the junk yard dog of Christianity to a fight. Well to say the least I walked out of there unharmed, yet I had created a nemesis for my soul who would critique me and my limited knowledge of the Bible every chance he got.

The prison church is no different than the so called Free Church. It's divided and split amongst the Baptist, the Protestants and the Catholics and everyone thinks everyone else is wrong and they're right. In which case I actually don't want to be right, I want to be changed! I want to experience God, not religion! I want to see men and women set free by the power of Jesus Christ! Religion never frees us it only brings us into greater bondage. Fortunately for me I was an ex-thug whose only images of church were of Easter egg hunts at Eagle Wing Baptist Church under the leadership of Pastor Henry O. Maxwell. I didn't know what it meant to be dogmatic! So I was open to a move of God not to mention I had been delivered from demons literally. It was too late to tell me that demons and the Holy Spirit weren't real! I had experienced both and for you to attack men who had taught me things about the Spirit of God and that helped revolutionize my thinking concerning spiritual truths, you were crazy. I would rather have a little wild fire and fanaticism as others would say than for me to believe God doesn't heal, deliver, or set free. It was too late to take my wild fire, label me with the "name it" and "claim it" crew. All I knew was, I was once lost but now I'm found. I was once blind and now I see. And my sight came way of the crazimatics, I mean, charismatics. I was Word of Faith and there was nothing he or anyone else could say to change that.

Milan was amazing for ministry. We had churches coming in every Monday night under the leadership of Momma. Momma was a prison ministry legend. She was in charge of bringing in her ministry and others to minister to the men and boy did she bring me in. I didn't fully understand anointed preaching but I had encountered the anointing at different levels. The people Momma brought in were anointed, Straight Gate church had some anointed prophets and teachers who would have you in there shouting out of your shoes. One man got to preaching so hard he just started laying hands on men without a catcher. Folks were falling like flies and I knew I was too cool to fall. Next thing I know I'm on the ground stuck to the floor trying to get up and couldn't! I fell under the power and I was like wow ... God is amazing!

My favorite ministry that would come into the prison house was First Baptist of Roseville under the leadership of Pastor Lenneld Caldwell. This brother and his ministry team came in and did skits and led us in worship and ministered the word so powerfully. I was in awe of their presentation of the gospel. It was alive energetic and entertaining and it didn't hurt that they brought a few young ladies that were easy on the eyes. The prison was always packed when they came and not everyone who was coming had Jesus on their mind. Milan was a powerful time of growing in the things of God! The Lord made me the chaplain's clerk and I assisted by passing out Bibles and teaching tapes from behind my half door office. It was great I could sit and listen to teaching tapes all day. I was so hungry for the Word I would take teaching series and transcribe them to paper so I could study them back at the dorm. I would also take those same tapes and teach them in a class the Lord had opened up for me to teach on Tuesdays. I was in Bible training school for the Lord and it was awesome beyond anything I could have ever imagined! God was training me for ministry. My schedule was busy! I was in the drug program in the morning, working at the prison chapel and working out in the weight room while dreaming about the doors being opened to go home. While life was as good as it could get in prison, it was also challenging. I had completed the drug program. The program was very difficult at times not so much the content but the counselors. Some of them hated to see you go it seemed because they found petty reasons daily to reassess your file and try to get you kicked out of the drug program. However, I had made it, barely, and my barely had nothing to do with the program or the counselors it had everything to do with unchecked flesh and unresolved anger in me.

My roommate, for some odd reason, the closer I got to being finished with the program the more he would say and do things that would always start arguments. It was like he didn't want me to leave before him. I don't remember how it all got started but I'm two weeks from going home. Excitement is in the air when all of a sudden out of nowhere my roommate got up this false courage to challenge my manhood which caused him to come in contact with some flurry of blows and caused him to run up out of the room. I remember the fear like it was yesterday. You blew it, it's over you're going to the hole, you're not going home you're losing your 18 months off all in the name of an attitude! When my roommate ran out of the room I did my best Carl Lewis to catch him but on one leg I was limited in my mobility. I just knew he was going to turn me in. I prepared for the officers to come and to take me away at any moment; only a few hours later to have my roommate come back and I apologized every way an apology could be given! I told him "I don't know what came over me, I'm sorry the devil made me do it." Flip Wilson would have been proud of the abundance of excuses I made dealing with the issues of my flesh. He forgave me; I graduated from the class within three days and was released from Milan. My friend, Sean, picked me up outside of the prison doors. I walked to the car in disbelief. It had been nearly 6 years since I had seen the outside streets as a free man. I will never forget the ride back as I stared at the trees and the sky. Everything was so beautiful on the highway back to Cleveland, tears fell from my face as he drove I was free at last.

Chapter 15 - Freedom (Everything Had Changed)

I was 228 pounds standing 6 foot 3 with muscles bulging out of my polo shirts. When I left I was the same height but 350 pounds so people would walk passed me who knew me at my former weight in the natural. I had lost a whole person. Being thin and trim had its absolute advantages. I felt better; my back didn't hurt as bad. I was more agile on my feet. My clothes fit better and the ladies loved cool K. What a struggle to live right! I had never known the pressure men or women faced in trying to live Holy unto the Lord. I had made up in my mind I was going to be celibate. I would never make mistakes again. I was going to be the saint of all times. Never totally understanding prison is much different than the streets. There was nothing about another man in prison that I wanted so it was easy to be celibate and perfectly on fire for Jesus. Now I'm free and I have an air of invincibility about my walk with God. I'll never forget my best friend Damon's conversation about what I was about to face in the real world. He said let me help you with your super sanctified self. You are about to see things that you didn't see when you went away. People dress differently; women barely wear any clothes in the summer days! People are into threesomes, everyone is high on marijuana and sex is not hard at all to get. I said "Damon I don't want to hear all of that, I'm sold out to Jesus and I would never compromise my walk unto the Lord." His closing statement that day was please don't you forget, God saved you and before He saved you He knew you were going to make some mistakes! When you make your mistakes know that He knew it and still saw fit to save you.

EVERYTHING HAS CHANGED!

The marathon was on. Everywhere I turned I was in culture shock! I hadn't seen such beauty. I had never seen so many beautiful women in Cleveland. They didn't wait on a conversation they brought the conversation to you. I was amazed because I grew up in an era where you pursued the women! Now I had come home and the women were the pursuers. I stood strong at every test. I was a Christian saved and sanctified and filled with the Holy Spirit, until I met a young lady in a doctor's office that used a different approach. She didn't chase me she just looked at me with a dreamy stare and turned her attention back to her work. She didn't seem to be affected by my body or my beauty, at least she played like she wasn't but I was affected by her class and her beauty. The door was opened and the infatuation began. We started out with the movies and dinner almost every other day and when suddenly things got heated I began to visit her home unsupervised. At first it was cool. I was able to contain myself but as the Bible asks "can a man take fire into his bosom not get burnt?" I was beginning to weaken. I wasn't following my spirit on the inside. I was birthing something in the natural that seemed so right but James makes it so plain the process of how trouble is birthed into our lives!

James 1:14-15; But every man is tempted, when he is drawn away of his own lust, and enticed.
15; Then when lust hath conceived, it bringeth forth sin: and sin, when it is finished, bringeth forth death.

Death doesn't always mean that you physically die! Death, in my case, was I was beginning to die spiritually, my prayer life waned. My word life was at an all time low. I was saved, yes, but I was a struggling saint. The relationship was liberating for the woman in question. She had been in a very abusive relationship with a man who had Norman Bates- type characteristics. He was psycho to say the least. He had a history of hurting women physically and on this particular day I wasn't going to play the hero I was just stopping by to see my Boo! When I arrived I thought the gentleman was the gardener or a handy man when I spoke and walked passed. The gent he looked up at me with fire in his eyes. He moved quickly to where we were and began to declare whose house this was and how he was her man. Now forgive me for sounding crazy. She had left him years earlier but in his mind the relationship never ended and like most veterans of war he was still holding on to memories of his past. He jumped bad in the kitchen and I'm sure in times past he ran off many a man who had liked the fair lady but on this day as he screamed and went into his tantrum and acted like he was Kong I stood up from my seat and I got my nose close to his. I looked him in his eye and I said **----- you** may have beaten women in your past, but today you have come up against a real man. So we need to stop all of this talking and let's make it do what it do! I have never seen such courage turn into such cowardice, Kong gently changed his tone of voice and lowered his position. He walked out of that door as a defeated woman beater at least for this young lady he would never ever again threaten her with violence! That didn't mean he stopped pursuing her because he was obsessed and with good reason. She was a winner! However he realized she had a man that would at least defend his temporal territory. Life was changing fast for a super saint. I was on the spiritual decline even though I was going to church and still trying to pray, I was becoming much calloused in my spirit. Sin will cause your conscience to become seared. 1st Timothy 4:2; Speaking lies in hypocrisy; having their conscience seared with a hot iron;

I was becoming desensitized to sin and starting to lower God's standards for my life. Things were changing. I was back in the restaurant business. I had created a new style of cooking called a new kind of Cajun! People were coming from everywhere. We were growing at a faster rate than we could handle which caused great stress. Orders were coming in from hospitals, and we were making promises that we would deliver in a timely manner. The quick growth coupled with an understaffed, undertrained team was a recipe for disaster. What should have been celebratory times became stressful because now, too much business turned into not enough business because people got tired of waiting an hour for their food.

I will never forget that during my transition I would attend the legendary Christian fellowship under the leadership of Apostle Bill McKinney. I would always go there knowing that when the spirit got to moving the prophets would begin to speak. I knew I would be exposed for my error in spite of the prophetic truth that would cut me to pieces. I really enjoyed their worship service and the word that the Bishop would bring was always encouraging and motivating not to mention they brought in the best speakers from around the country. This Sunday was no exception. Phil Driscoll was in town and Bishop had brought me to the altar to testify about my deliverance in prison and my call to ministry. I testified to the goodness of God. He is called Faithful and True. I was the one struggling with trying to be a Christian, a business man and a boyfriend. When my testimony was over I sat down and Mr. Driscoll got up to sing and play. He was flowing and the spirit of God was high in that place when all of a sudden Mr. Driscoll stopped singing and playing and he looked and pointed at me and said, “Young man come quickly.” I looked around like who me! And he said “yes you.” I walked to the altar area not knowing what he wanted. I broke out in a cold sweat. He began to prophesy to me about my destiny, my calling; he finished with, “And God said you will not be in the fish business for long because he has called you to be a fisher of men!”

Rom 2:4 The goodness of God leadeth thee to repentance? Prophet Driscoll's words were etched into my soul and I could not sleep comfortably in sin. My heart was torn up! All that God had done for me, my great deliverance, being baptized in His spirit and now for me to come home and to bring shame to His kingdom, I was outdone with myself. I remember going to see my probation officer asking him for permission to attend Bible College. I had made God a promise before I left prison. I told him within a year of being home I would go to Bible school. I hate that I didn't tell him within 60 days of being home I would go to Bible College. A year was just enough time to almost derail my purpose in God. I nearly got caught up in a web the enemy had so deceitfully orchestrated in order to abort my life in God. I will never forget the mercy of God during this short but painful time in my life as the super saint came to the realization it truly is by Grace I was saved not of works. There was no place for my boasting, it was all God. Favor came supernaturally. God worked it out with the probation office. They agreed to let me move to Tulsa Oklahoma to attend the school of my dreams. I had filled out the application. I was just waiting for their response. It came on the best of all days. I was at the restaurant playing cook. No one showed up. I was at the grill sweating like I had went ten rounds with Mike Tyson when the phone rang and it was Rhema's admissions department. They called and said "Mr. Johnson you have been accepted into Rhema Bible training Center." I remember going back to the grill and asking myself two questions. Do you want this money? Or do you want your joy back? That day I chose joy. I could not see myself going another year in this state. Oklahoma here I come!

Chapter 16 - Training Time Is Never Wasted Time.

I was packed and ready to go! My family had thrown me a goodbye party, and God had supernaturally paid my tuition for several months. I was set, my Lexus was packed down, Oklahoma here I come. I was headed to the highway when I pulled over at the parks at Lake Erie and I was having second thoughts. I didn't know anyone in Oklahoma. Fear began to grip me and now I couldn't see leaving my friend behind. I sat there looking into space my mind racing about all I was giving up. I couldn't do it. I turned around and went to my friend's house for the evening. I woke up in the morning more determined than ever to get into the perfect will of God for my life. I proceeded to the highway. I began to pray and to seek God while driving down the highway. I got a breakthrough entering into Indianapolis. I begin to sing in my spirit and a peace flooded my soul. I couldn't get to Tulsa quickly enough. I made it after spending the night in a Missouri hotel jumping up at the crack of dawn and racing down the highway in a hurry to get to my new life. I was pulled over doing a hundred miles an hour. With ticket in hand, warning given, I slowed down somewhat. I pulled into Tulsa not knowing the makeup of the city. I stayed at a motel near the school in a city that looked like Mayberry. I was dumbfounded at what I had gotten myself into. The next day I registered in school and paid part of my tuition. I was in awe of the school and the church. I had never seen such excellence in ministry. I was blown away, I was at Rhema. During orientation God gave me some wonderful friends. They showed me that Tulsa was more than Mayberry. It was a spiritual Mecca that offered absolute change.

For the next two years I would experience the most fun, spiritual growth and pain a person could go through surrendering their life to the Lord. Rhema was awesome! The teachers were incredible, they made learning fun. The Holy Spirit moved in our services. God was breathing on us not to mention Gods best friend was there in Brother Hagin teaching us classes periodically, I was in Heaven. School was exciting. I looked forward to being there daily; it was when school let out that I had the most trouble. I had connected with a group of men and women from the school who loved to party. We never drank or smoke we just ate and went to the movies all of the time. I did my best to stay clear of any relationships. I didn't want to lose my focus again! I had gotten my joy back. Somehow another female student slid in under me, it was about 12 of us at a local restaurant having a good time and we all exchanged numbers. Never thinking it was really a ploy for some to have contact information on others. Until one day I'm at home studying, I get a call from a female student asking me if I could take her to work. At first I was like no, but my heart smote me, I could give another Christian a ride and keep it platonic. The ride to her job was quiet because I know me. The moment we start talking freely and casually it's going to open up the door to other things. Except this time I met a woman who would not compromise her walk with God, our friendship was just that a real Christian friendship. We dated for a short time. She taught me you could be in a relationship and not have sex. I will forever be grateful to this woman of God for her integrity. She said no when both of our bodies were saying yes. But during some of the toughest times I would face in Bible College God used her to be a prayer partner and a support system as I faced many trials going through school. God used her to pray down power and peace from heaven. An occasional meal at her hands and gas fill ups never hurt. God provided in a multitude of ways while I was at school. I am forever indebted to the various people God used. Two incidents that I want to highlight or rather two people. Brother Roary and Pastor Doug Jones. God had placed these men in my life when it seemed like I was being forced to give up. I was riding down 71st street driving this beautiful Lexus that had absolutely no gas and I did not have a red nickel to my name. I could remember telling God I know you didn't bring me this far to leave me. I was pleading my case crying like I had just gotten a beating from my mother for being disobedient. The tears flowing ever so strongly I did my best to pull myself together before I pulled up on the grounds of the Rhema campus. I remember, brother Roary running up to my car and saying "Brother Ken would you drop me off to such and such a place. I will give you gas money." I have never told someone to get in as fast as I did Roary on that day. God answered my prayer that day he put enough gas in the car to last me a few days. Oh the faithfulness of God. At the same time I knew that I owed for that months tuition at the school and I did not have it. Unfortunately I didn't know anyone who did have it!

I prayed and left it in the hands of God. I remember time was running out and I was about to be kicked out of school for nonpayment of tuition. Then I had gotten a call to the administration office. I understood their terms and I humbly let them know I didn't have it but I believed God. I continued on in school for a few days and on my last day of eligibility I was sitting in the main auditorium for classes outside of the church when Doug Jones walked in and said Ken you won't be getting kicked out of school today. I paid your tuition. I didn't know how he knew but I was ever grateful to God! God used him and I cried tears of joy in the presence of God and Pastor Doug! God had done it again!

Chapter 17 - Queen Esther Is Being Called Home!

My first year was nearly up and the calls had begun to pour in from Cleveland! The woman who had raised me was near death. My grandmother had always meant a lot to me. She gave me a home as a child and she raised me in a stern way. It seemed the older she got, the sweeter she got. I had always been close to her and now she was succumbing to cancer which she had fought for years without treatment, but now it was taking its effect upon her. All of her daughters were giving her 24-hour care. I kept hearing their cry for me to come home and to see about the one who had raised me. I was torn wanting to be there for my grandmother and wanting to finish my first year at Rhema Bible Training Center. I decided to go to God in prayer and I prayed and asked God to keep my grandmother alive until this first year was finished. God honored that request. I walked into my grandmother's apartment the day I arrived back in Cleveland after completing my first year of Bible training. I went in to her bedroom and I remember looking at all the weight she had lost. Tears began to well up in me. As I sat there and talked with my grandmother she smiled at my presence as I held her hand and within a couple of days she was taken to the hospital where we would gather as a family as she crossed from time to eternity. I am so glad that God had had allowed me to go home prior to my grandmother's death. I had led my grandmother in the sinner's prayer on a previous visit. She had made her peace with God; she made her salvation sure through God's grace and her grandson's prayer. Mommy would be missed but she lives on through all of her daughters. I'll never forget her funeral. The word God gave me to minister was "She Ain't Dead and It Ain't Over." Many family members made a decision for Christ at her funeral and the scripture was fulfilled that declares unless a grain of wheat is sown into the ground and dies it cannot bring forth more fruit.

My second year of school was nowhere near as hard as the first! God opened up the flood gates financially and he did an overflowing work in my life. Every need was met. The God of too much had showed up and rewarded me for my faithfulness. During my second year I had my attorney file a petition with the courts asking that I be taken off the remaining 3 years of probation. The day of graduation, I got a call from my lawyer saying the petition had been granted by the court. I was free to move about as I pleased. It was like God was saying there will be no limits or restrictions placed upon your ministry. God was restoring everything in my life the devil had stolen God was making room for A new beginning. Graduation was powerful. Pastor Darryl Huffman preached "Don't be disobedient to the heavenly vision." The next morning I was slated to preach at the Gates of Refuge Church which was really a set up by God for marriage.

Chapter 18 - I Wish She Was Mine

I was sitting amongst the preachers nervously awaiting my introduction by the prophet. In the midst of waiting to minister I noticed a lady serving the pastors at the pulpit. She was absolutely breathtaking, the finest thing in Oklahoma I had seen. I paid close attention to her clothes, her hair, her mannerism, her pulpit etiquette. I said in my heart "Lord I wish that was my wife." For some odd reason I equated her with being one of the preachers wives who sat in the pulpit. That day I saw what I desired in a wife but for fear she was someone else's I gave her a somber hello not wanting to seem like I was courting another man's wife. It would be a couple of months before I would see Minister Carrie again. I was in the cafeteria of an office building that allowed vendors to come in and set up and sale various goods on payday. I remember selling goods with every ounce of salesmanship I could muster, when I heard a voice saying, "Hello Minister Ken." I looked to the voice and I saw the woman who I had desired at church speaking to me. I quickly responded "How are you and how is your husband doing?" She said, "What husband? I don't even have a boyfriend!" I said, "Hold up don't move we will be married in a few short weeks." I quickly called her pastor and her sister and asked for permission to begin the courting process. Within days it was confirmed in my heart that she was the one. I began quickly to cut out anything in my life that didn't look like an answer to prayer. We courted for months, dinner, movies, church, shopping, and countless hours on the telephone praying together and getting to know one another. The day came when I got up the courage to get her a ring that cost me all the money in America, I thought. I mustered up the courage to ask her sitting at a dinner table would she marry me ring in hand. After what seemed like an hour she said "Yes, I will marry you." Our hearts melted that day, our yes resounded into the heavens! We began to make plans to spend our life together. True love had come to pass and God was about to be glorified, at least that's what we thought.

Marriage is much more difficult than dating. When you date you're always on your best behavior. You dress differently when you date compared to when you're married, your manners are different. When you date you don't belch, you don't pass gas, you try to use soft tones when you're speaking. Dating is absolutely a fairy tale compared to marriage. We didn't live together so she really didn't know my household habits, I didn't know hers and we became one and joined all of our things as we merged. Our personalities, our families were merged and within a week we were saying or rather screaming I want a divorce. I know you're never suppose to use that language saved sanctified and filled with the Holy Spirit but we were about to literally kill one another. For some odd reason I thought when my wife was at home she was suppose to look like Barbie, keep the house clean like Mr. Belvedere and cook like G. Garvin! And my only duties were to go out and to bring home the money. So my twisted thinking caused hundreds of self inflicted arguments because I was making demands on her that no human could carry out. Do this, do that, dress this way and do your hair that way! Cook me this and that! I had a list of what she needed to be doing on a daily basis. I really wasn't looking for a wife and partnership I was looking for a maid I could have sex with. Unfortunately I met a woman who wasn't just happy to say I got a man. She was confident she wasn't having any form of disrespect and she wasn't going to keep quiet. Carrie spoke her mind and I hated every bit of it so we clashed daily, we never physically fought but we fought with our words and after having her walk out of the house literally barefoot and defiant on several occasions, we sat down and talked about the issues. I gave her a list as long as any kings scroll of all of the things she could do better she being the virtuous women she is! She had her list of all of these outright lies and areas I needed to change in so I thought! The breakthrough came when we both decided to stop praying to God about the other's issues and I started praying Lord change Me. If she never changes or bows to all of my wishes God give me the grace to stay with the wife you gave me. Unbeknownst to me, she was in the other room crying out to God to be broken, she wasn't praying about this man any longer and his ways she began to pray to God for change within her. Through all of this brokenness and change God gave us a child. Carrie was pregnant with Christen and somewhere in the middle of all the chaos and prayers we both began to grow up. We realized love wasn't just a feeling it was a commitment. We recommitted ourselves to our marriage and we recommitted ourselves to the Lord. Day by day we grew closer and the love we had for our daughter and our family intensified the love we had in our marriage. Thank God for mercy, grace and the long suffering of God. One thing I learned from the beginning of our marriage was, if you move to quickly you can throw away a treasure sent from heaven. We have to learn how to fight for our marriages, and not just fight for the sake of fighting, fight until we win in marriage.

A year earlier I had decided it was time to leave Tulsa and to go and plant Gods church. I had made up in my mind that God could not survive unless I went and opened up a church in the great city of East Cleveland, Ohio. I was zealous but not according to knowledge. My marriage had great struggles. In the natural it didn't look like we were going to make it! But I was Word of Faith and it didn't matter how my wife felt, the Word says *Luke 18:29-30;*

> *29 And he said unto them, Verily I say unto you, There is no man that hath left house, or parents, or brethren, or wife, or children, for the kingdom of God's sake,*
>
> *30 Who shall not receive manifold more in this present time, and in the world to come life everlasting.*

I had made up in my mind I was gone and I had a word from the Lord to back me up. In my mind I thought I was right to think that way but in my heart my decision never set well in my spirit. I always had uneasiness in my spirit that forced me to pray out the plan of God. It was through much prayer and study of the word that I came to the realization that God didn't give me a wife so I could then divorce her, start a church and it was all for His Glory. God gave me peace that at the right time my wife would know and I would know that it was time to move. So we kept working for the Lord and working at Mr. Wonderfuls our clothing store and we kept working on improving our marriage. I realize today that divorcing my wife would have been the worst mistake I ever could have made because not only is she a great wife she is an incredible mother and powerful minister of the Gospel of Jesus Christ. During my time of waiting on the Lord I sought the Lord in prayer about our church name and its structure how we were to operate. God gave me revelation on every area, not to mention I was an excellent observer of what worked in great churches and what didn't. So preparation time and training time is never wasted time.

The Prophet Speaks.

It was Sunday afternoon. Church was already over. I had met my responsibility as a Christian and now it was time to chill, eat big and watch a football game. Then the phone rang, it was Apostle Carter inviting me to a Sunday night service with a guest speaker by the name of Dr. Cindy Trimm. He insisted that we be there. I said yes reluctantly. I didn't want to go to church again that day. I had already given the Lord his day, but out of respect for the apostle I forced my way on to service. The worship was high, the anointing was getting thicker by the moment, and the guest speaker was brought to the altar area as she began to pray. I sensed an uncommon anointing; God was with this woman, as she began to speak of things pertaining to the Kingdom of God. I was blown away plus she had a delivery that was strong like T.D. Jakes. I was overwhelmed by the revelation and power in which Dr. Trimm demonstrated through the Word of God! The place was on fire, people were shouting and crying and the spirit of God was moving. Suddenly Dr. Trimm called for a line for the pastors of the city or those who were in ministry or about to get in ministry. I had heard her in my spirit but my mind kept telling me no you don't even have a church yet, but my spirit kept telling me and my wife to go. We got up the courage and walked down the aisle to get to the altar, we were at the end of the line when Dr. Trimm looked at us and said you two come first. God's word really is true, the last shall be first.

Dr. Trimm gave her instructions to the pastors, "if I don't have anything I'm not going to make up something I think you want to hear nor will the prophets in training speak out of turn if they don't hear or see anything then you just keep walking through the line." The prophets in training were our first stop they gave us a good word nothing flaky or anything but a very confirming word. Our next stop was before Dr. Trimm, she began to speak to my wife about her calling and how she didn't want to go to this place, but God had been dealing with her heart and how that God was going to use her in a supernatural way. Dr. Trimm Spoke about how the apostle and the prophet would work together to bring about glorious change. She then began to look at me and began to describe the area I was called to and how that God was going to use us to bring great light into an area filled with darkness.

The prophecy was very intense, the congregants were shouting for what God was speaking over our lives and we began to walk back off the stage to our seats when all of a sudden Dr. Trimm begins to shout at us "I see train loads coming, I see train loads coming, resources coming into your life for ministry, I see train loads and its coming like a locomotive. I see it." She said 'God is going to bless you, governments will come and seek you" the prophecy was strong. Today we have seen parts of it come to pass naturally and the rest coming to pass super naturally because in our hearts everything the prophet said was true is true and has happened. So we patiently wait for the manifestation of all things. A few days after the prophetic service my wife came to me and declared she was ready to make the move. God had shifted her heart, plus our marriage was much stronger than it was a year earlier; the timing of God had come to pass. Wait on the Lord and again I say wait Psalm 27: 1 Wait on the LORD: be of good courage, and he shall strengthen thine heart: wait, I say, on the LORD.

Chapter 19 - The Planting Of The Church

In school we were taught in planting a church for the Lord to consider everything, doing your demographics, income and location are very important. When planting a church in the natural and the spiritual those things are true but at the end of the day where God guides, he will provide. I began to come back to Cleveland flying on the weekends looking for a place we could at least call our temporary home. I came for a few weeks without any success except for a number of hall rentals in a city called East Cleveland. I knew that this wasn't where I was supposed to be, not East Cleveland. It had been through a very rough transition, once a prominent suburb which was now devastated by drugs and crime not to mention in times past I was a part of the problem. But I knew God wasn't calling me to come back to that place to now be a part of the solution. Boy was I wrong for some odd reason I kept getting this prompting to call the phone number off the building but I had lost the number on purpose and had to have someone go and retrieve the number for me again off the building. I called, set up the appointment to see the hall which was owned by another church. At the end of the day we rented there temporarily. To say the least, I thank God for the experience in the building. It was a very interesting partnership which made us stronger as a church family. There came a time when we would be put out of there for paying our rent on time. The pastor had gotten upset with our church because we had gotten a contract to purchase the old vacant supermarket right next door. For some odd reason, that didn't sit well with the pastor we were renting from and the next thing we knew, we were forced to move out of a place that we were paying a hundred dollars an hour to rent and was never late with a payment. Being forced to find another place in the area was a tough task but I felt God was calling us to relocate to my basement and in the basement we found out who was really called to this local church.

The Trials

Many people left the church during this critical transition. A lot of people told us to call them when we got a building because they didn't fill comfortable worshiping in a basement. It was all good; God was in control. We kept moving forward preaching the gospel and loving people. When the smoke clears, it's Gods church it's not ours. Church is His idea; I just want to be found faithful doing the masters will. The basement church was beautiful painful and needed.

God had other plans on His mind. Finally we had a contract in hand for a new building, keys to go in it and prepare it for interior demolition before we transferred the deed. We began to clean up and tear out everything in the building every Saturday for weeks. We were having demolition BBQ's. We had grills blaring outside and people working inside; team work was making the dream work. God brought in resources from everywhere imaginable people were throwing money in a bucket riding past the building. They were stopping by buying barbeque dinners. Home Depot gave us a few gift cards. The member's sacrificed, church members were writing checks and God was getting the glory. We truly never had big lumps of money but every week we took what we had and invested into our house. The grand opening came on a blistery winter night. We had the nerve to have a guest speaker in a building that didn't have sufficient heat. We had an over head heater that seemed like it was blowing out cold air. We never felt its heat, we had some kerosene heaters burning and they were literally toxic. Everybody in church had a headache but we pushed forward.

No carpet on the floor, we actually painted them black the day we had our first service. Because we didn't have proper heat in the building, the walls were still wet; they were so wet that when I walked past the walls to go and sit at my seat, paint was all over my coat.

But we had a building, everything else was minor. God would work out the minute details over time. We had a place called home. The service that night was powerful. We were shaking, shivering and shouting unto the Lord. He had given us victory one more time; Life Changers International Church had a building a place we could call home. Glory be to God!

The Vision

Church is very interesting especially when people know your past. I have always been very transparent about what God delivered me from. I let our members know you are going to hear some stories about me and yes most of them will be true. In my past I did a lot of wrong, I hurt a lot of people, I sold a lot of drugs, I abused a lot of good women who didn't deserve it but like Paul after having his encounter with Christ and understanding his righteousness Paul said 2nd Corinthians 7:1-2; Having therefore these promises, dearly beloved, let us cleanse ourselves from all filthiness of the flesh and spirit, perfecting holiness in the fear of God. 2; Receive us; we have wronged no man, we have corrupted no man, we have defrauded no man.

Paul said we have wronged no man. This coming from a Christian killer, how could Paul make that statement? The only way he could say he has done no evil was because of his relationship with the Lord Jesus Christ. Paul understood God had wiped away all of his sins and in Christ he was absolutely a brand new man

2nd Corinthians 5:17; Therefore if any man be in Christ, he is a new creature: old things are passed away; behold all things are become new.

People may not understand it, but today I have wronged no man. I am made brand new by the blood of the Lord Jesus Christ. In my past I did a lot of wrong but today I walk in the newness of life. Christ paid the ultimate price for my sins and for every person's sins that will ever walk on this planet and today I choose to live from his finished work. Jesus paid the price and I can't even pay the tip. In East Cleveland I am responsible for preaching the gospel of Jesus Christ to every creature. Some family and some friends may not get it because they know me in the flesh. Jesus gives every believer a warning concerning this and if we are smart we will take heed and create kingdom strategies to win people and regions who don't know you! Amongst your family and friends you may not do many great exploits.

Mark 6:4-6

4; But Jesus said unto them, a prophet is not without honor, but in his own country, and among his own kin, and in his own house.

5 And he could there do no mighty work, save that he laid His hands upon a few sick fold and healed them

6 And he marveled because of their unbelief. And he went around about the villages, teaching.

Even Jesus couldn't do many miracles except heal a few colds and headaches. Why? Because of familiarity. Isn't that Joseph's boy? The people around them missed out on their miracles and deliverance because all they could see is who they thought they knew. So they lived from a past familiarity which blocked them from receiving the anointing that was on His life. If the people from Jesus' own home town couldn't receive him, I asked the Lord, how then will I be successful in my hometown and He answered it in the same passage of scripture.

Mark 6:6-13

And he went round about the villages, teaching.

7 And he called unto Him the twelve, and began to send them forth by two and two; and gave them power over unclean spirits;

8 And commanded them that they should take nothing for their journey, save a staff only; no script, no bread, no money in their purse:

9 But be shod with sandals; and not put on two coats.

10 And he said unto them, In what place so ever ye enter into an house, there abide till ye depart from that place.

11: And whosoever shall not receive you, nor hear you, when ye depart thence, shake off the dust under your feet for a testimony against them. Verily I say unto you, It shall be more tolerable for Sodom and Gomorrah in the Day of Judgment, than for that city.

12: And they went out, and preached that men should repent.

13: And they cast out many devils, and anointed with oil many that were sick, and healed them.

Jesus didn't let the people's unbelief stop him from being effective in ministry. The answer to unbelief is in strong teaching, but besides teaching discipleship is the answer. Notice Jesus had a core of people who believed in Him. Jesus trained them, spent time with them, he transferred power to them and then he sent them out two by two so that they could win the world in His Name. Sheep have to beget other sheep especially when people are always trying to smite the Shepherd. I want to encourage pastors and saints who are on fire and serving amongst family and friends in your own home town. Keep teaching; rise up undeniable disciples, people who have a passion and fervor for God. Some may be able to say, I know you but when they see strong disciples being produced who have a testimony of the delivering power of God, when they see them changed and healed it won't be long before they come from all around to receive a touch from God. I'm watching God touch a lot of lives through the members of Life Changers. When they bring people its people who could care less about what they say about me from my past. They want to meet the man who helped to change their neighborhood or to help get their son or daughter off of crack.

God has been faithful to me and my family. He has been faithful to our local church, even in the midst of great adversity. We have seen so much in such a short period of time, but through every trial God has given us victory. The flesh has cried many of nights on the shoulders of God but I've found that God is a good listener and also an outstanding healer. At the end of the day its God's church. They are His people. All I can do is be faithful to him and to love them. People will be people. One day they sing your praises, the next day they crucify you. But God never changes. He actually says in his word: Heb 13:8 Jesus Christ the same yesterday, and today, and forever.

God is an awesome God! Today I'm focused on pleasing Him, following Him, living my best life for Him. I truly can say I love a man named Jesus who died for my sins, He changed my life, He gave me all of my hearts desires and has been faithful through every storm. I don't know where you're at in your life but I want to introduce you to a friend who will stick closer to you than a brother. He has healing for Your Soul. His name is Jesus. He is the son of God who came to earth in a man's body to pay the eternal price for sinful man. Jesus declares in *John 11:25-26 I am the resurrection, and the life: he that believeth in me, though he was dead, yet shall he live:26 And whosoever liveth and believeth In me shall never die. Believest thou this?* Jesus will give you eternal life. Inwardly you will become brand new in your spirit; your flesh will look the same. If you were bald before Jesus came into your heart you will be bald after wards. Jesus will make your spirit brand new. He will cause you by an act of your will to be born again. It doesn't matter what you have done, how many sins you have committed in your life. The blood of Jesus will wipe away all of your Sins and will cause you to become born again.

The Prayer of Champions

Pray this simple prayer with me: Lord Jesus come into my heart, I believe that You died for my sins and that You rose again so I could live again today! Lord Jesus I confess You as my personal Lord and Savior and I believe with all of my heart You are the son of God and I confess your Lordship over my life. Lord Jesus take my life and use it for Your glory! Amen!

My friend if you prayed that prayer from your heart, you just got born again. The next step is for you to chase after God. Read His word daily, pray to the Father in Jesus name; get in a good Bible believing church that's on fire for God. And when you make a mistake, stay in the love of God. Confess your sins and ask God to give you power to overcome your areas of weakness. I would rather make a mistake with Jesus than to make mistakes without Him. We love you in the Lord. God bless you, and thanks for taking time out of your schedule to read this life-changing book.

Your brother in Christ,
Pastor Kenneth W. Johnson
Check out our services online at: www.lcchurch.us
Email me personally your praise reports and your prayers at pkjohnson71@gmail.com!

Pastor Ken Johnson is the Senior Pastor of Life Changers Church in the city of East Cleveland, Ohio, where he serves with his wife, First Lady Carrie Johnson. They are the proud parents of Aubrey, Christa, Christen, Kaelin and Moses, and a host of spiritual sons and daughters. Pastor Ken Johnson was touched by the Hand of God in a Chapel service where he went looking for change and in the process got more than he bargained for as he received salvation, and deliverance from demonic spirits by the Power of God. Literally Demons came out of him screaming and hollering at the name of Jesus. God delivered him in that service and instantly baptized him with the Holy Spirit and for 2 hours Pastor Ken sang in a heavenly Language that he had never spoken in before. That night his Life was changed forever by the Power of God. Pastor Ken ministers under a strong teaching and preaching gift, with a special grace and anointing for teaching believers how to receive the Holy Spirit and learning to hear the voice of God. You can go online at www.lcchurch.us where you can watch archived messages, and live streaming of my services, or email me at pkjohnson71@gmail.com.and send in your prayer request which I pray for personally.

www.lcchurch.us
life changers 4ever

216-373-0879